The Organic Gospel

by
Gary C. Price
&
Maisha Hunter

Published by Remnant Publishing House
Atlanta, GA   30122

Printed in the United States of America

Unless otherwise noted, Scripture is from the King James Version.

For additional information about Omega Ministries, visit our website:

http://www.omegaministries.org

ISBN Number: 0-9714797-1-2

Acknowledgment

This book is due in large part to the members and partners of Omega Church and Ministries Center, Inc. You have faithfully believed in our dream, vision, and word from the Lord. You have supported this ministry financially and prayerfully over the years in the midst of extremely trying times.

A special acknowledgment must also be given to Tyson Ranes for translating this vision into art with his inspired graphics and the design of the book cover.

Thanks to all of you for your love and support in the preaching and teaching of the Gospel of our Lord Jesus Christ.

Dedication

With great joy I dedicate this book to my wife, Barbara, and our three kids Gary II, Gabriel, and Brejanae who have stood by me over the years and made my life one of joy, peace, and fun!
Pastor Gary C. Price

I dedicate this book to my husband, Vincent, whose strength and smile have always been a source of encouragement for me. Also to our children - Lauren, Alana, and Jordan - who teach me daily what love truly means.
Maisha Hunter

Table of Contents

Meet the Authors 9
Foreword 11
Chapter 1 - In The Beginning God 13
   Every Seed After Its Own Kind 13
   You Reap What You Sow 14
   The Woman's Seed & The Serpent's Seed 16
Chapter 2 - The Two Are Contrary One to the Other 21
   The Flesh Lusts Against the Spirit 21
   Separating the Wheat from the Tares 23
   Except A Seed Die 25
Chapter 3 - Seed Sown Amongst the Thorns 33
   Caught in the Weeds 33
   Defiled Fruit 37
Chapter 4 - Incorruptible Seed 61
   Seed Coming to Fruition 61
   The Seed is the Word of God 62
   You Shall Know Them by Their Fruit 64
   Organic Growth vs. Organized Flesh 66
   A Godly Seed 69
Chapter 5 - Break Up Your Fallow Ground 73
   Transformation vs. Performance 73
   Your Fruit Should Remain 76
   Extermination 79
   Cultivation 84
Chapter 6 - Transplanted for New Life 87
   New Soil 87
   The Axe is Laid to the Root 90
   A Pruning 95
   A Vine Out of Egypt 98
   The Fruit of Love 105
   The Harvest is Ripe 109
   Aaron's Rod Budding 113
Prayer 128

Meet the Authors

Gary C. Price

Pastor Gary C. Price is the Senior Pastor of Omega Church and Ministries Center located in Atlanta, Georgia. He has been ministering to the Body of Christ under an anointing that deals specifically with the bondage of the inner-man.

Pastor Price believes that the present day Church has lost the vision that Jesus Christ imparted to the Apostles before He departed to be enthroned with His Father. He also believes that the Church must be brought to repentance and humility through self denial in order for God to move in these last days. When listening to his words many have received the revelations of a prophetic voice calling the Church back to patriarchal authority and obedience to the Holy Spirit.

His ministry began in 1984 after God prophetically called him to remove barriers that Satan has constructed to separate God from His people. The main barrier to be removed, he believes, is religious bondage to man-centered organizations. He has diligently sought the Lord for guidance on how to go about initiating the end-time deliverances to set the Body of Christ free.

Maisha Hunter

Maisha Hunter is a wife and mother of three who writes regularly for The Latter Days Ministry blog. She also spent 10 years as co-owner of the Christian publishing company, Remnant Publishing House.

Raised as a devout Roman Catholic, Maisha committed herself to participating in the sacraments and being an active parishioner. Yet all of these religious works gave her no power to cease from sin and brought her no closer to truly knowing the Lord.

Tired of the hypocrisy and perversion in her own life and in the Catholic Church at large, she cried out in desperation to the Lord and said, "If this is the Church, then I am better off in the world. God, if you are real then I am asking you to reveal yourself to me. If you don't, then I might just stop believing altogether." God answered her prayer.

The Lord led her to purchase a Bible as well as other resources, and the Holy Spirit began to open her eyes to His word as she began to study the Scriptures. Since that time, Jesus has taken her on a journey to learn the difference between bondage to religion versus liberty through relationship with Him. Where the Spirit of the Lord is, there is liberty.

Foreword

A mystery made simple and understandable is absolutely incredible. What's even more incredible is that we have this mystery captured in the pages of this book.

The Organic Gospel is an absolute must read for believers that are seeking to do the will of God.

I don't know of anyone more suited (or fitted) to write on this topic than Gary and Maisha. Ever since I've known them, they've been consistent, authentic and sincere. I believe that's because they are the fruit of what's written on these pages.

This book reveals the truth behind spiritual growth and development in the life of the Christian.

Rashid Tillis
Disciple of Christ Jesus

Chapter 1 - In The Beginning, God...

Every Seed After Its Own Kind

> *Genesis 1:1-5*
> *In the beginning God created the heaven and the earth.*
> *And the earth was without form, and void; and darkness*
> *was upon the face of the deep. And the spirit of God moved*
> *upon the face of the waters. And God said, Let there be*
> *light: and there was light. And God saw the light, that it*
> *was good: and God divided the light from the darkness.*
> *And God called the light Day, and the darkness he called*
> *Night. And the evening and the morning were the first day.*

These opening Scriptures outline the beginning of all creation as the triune Godhead came together to create what we know today as the earth. Genesis, which means the beginning or starting point of conception, is the book of the Bible which outlines these sequences.

From start to finish - **Genesis to Revelation** - the Bible is written in an *organic* format as it outlines how God interacts with us. It reveals how every work of God goes through a pattern of conception, gestation, and manifestation. The end is not revealed from the beginning; rather God takes creation through a growth process before manifesting His desired result.

Creation was a complete and perfect work when God finished it. Yet, the entirety of what God was after is not visible from the beginning. God initially created Adam and Eve, but His desire was for them to multiply and establish the human race across the whole earth.

> *Genesis 1:28*
> *And God blessed them, and God said unto them [referring*
> *to Adam and Eve], Be fruitful, and multiply, and replenish*
> *the earth, and subdue it: and have dominion over the fish of*
> *the sea, and over the fowl of the air, and over every living*
> *thing that moveth upon the earth.*

The Bible itself opens with an illustration of God's organic work in the earth. He plants, cultivates, gestates, and in due time brings forth the full manifestation of what was first planted. Similarly, God has taken all of civilization through periods of gestation - different time frames and parameters - so that He may establish a new kingdom where His Son, Jesus Christ, is Lord. This kingdom is being *organically grown* out of the hearts of human beings on a global scale. My friends, for you to understand God's mind, it is important for you to know that the Gospel itself is organic.

> *Galatians 4:19*
> *My little children, of whom I travail in birth again until Christ be formed in you.*

The Gospel of Jesus Christ is designed to be planted within you and go through periods of gestation until Christ manifests out of you. Jesus said that the kingdom of God is not something to be observed outside of you because it is growing organically within; deep down in the very nature of your being.

> *Luke 17:20-21*
> *And when he was demanded of the Pharisees, when the kingdom of God should come, he answered them and said, The kingdom of God cometh not with observation: neither shall they say, Lo here! Or, lo there! For, behold, the kingdom of God is within you.*

You Reap What You Sow

As we approach the culmination of the age, gestation periods are coming to an end. Both the sons of God and the sons of Satan are coming to maturity for imminent manifestation and also **confrontation**. Therefore, we must examine ourselves carefully to see just what seed has been sown into our hearts (2 Corinthians 13:5).

What do we really believe? What nature has taken control of us (Galatians 5:19-23)? Is it the nature and character of the Lord Jesus Christ as evidenced by the fruit of the Spirit: love, joy, peace, longsuffering, gentleness, goodness, meekness, temperance, and faith? Or is it the satanic seed, with its seventeen works of the flesh showing forth the nature of the devil? Will we show ourselves to be the seed of Christ or the seed of the serpent?

> *Genesis 1:11-12*
> *And God said, Let the earth bring forth grass, the herb yielding seed, and the fruit tree yielding fruit after his kind, whose seed is in itself, upon the earth: and it was so. And*

*the earth brought forth grass, and herb yielding seed after
his kind, and the tree yielding fruit whose seed was in itself,
after his kind: and God saw that it was good.*

In these last days, both kingdoms will come to fruition as the life
within each of us is revealed for what it is. Remember, each seed produces
after its own kind; apple seeds produce apple trees; orange seeds produce
orange trees; and so on. All seed-bearing fruit produces the same lineage
of that which was sown.

Consider yourself. Your characteristics are a reflection of the seed sown
into your mother by your father. Perhaps your hands resemble your mother's,
or your nose is like your father's. There is always some resemblance in the
offspring testifying to the fact that it comes from the genetic makeup of
its parents. Your parents' genetic code *biologically* imprints upon you as
evidence that you were conceived by them. As it is on the physical plane,
so it is on the spiritual.

Spirits also have the ability to imprint their personalities upon the souls
of men, encoding their nature into the vessels through which they live. The
realm of the spirit is a reproductive arena as spirits replicate their character
in men. This is how spirit begets spirit (John 3:6). Whether lust, fear, greed...
whatever the spirit, the character traits of that spirit will manifest in that
person. By discerning the fruits, you can then see what spirit is housed
in a human being. In this way, both God's and the Devil's kingdoms are
organically grown. Each must be meticulously watered, nurtured, and fed
in order to grow. After this gestation period, the seed which has been sown
is brought to full stature for manifestation.

Believe me; the Devil is neither careless nor ignorant. He is working
methodically to replicate himself in the human character by perverting,
diluting, and rendering helpless the human mind. As this happens, man
will *by nature* have a stronger desire for that which is profane. This is what
Satan accomplished in the Garden of Eden when he tempted Adam and
Eve into sin.

Genesis 1:27
*So God created man in his own image, in the image of God
created he him; male and female created he them.*

Man was created in God's image to have dominion over the earth,
ruling it in God's stead. However, through deception and distortion of truth,
Satan was able to lead mankind into perversion and rebellion against his
Creator. This rebellion allowed Satan's very nature to be conceived in the

human mind and heart. Man's mind then became anti-God and anti-Christ; making him God's enemy (Colossians 1:21). God responded to this rebellion by casting Adam and Eve out of Eden and pronouncing a curse on them and Satan, so as to separate these entities from His presence. Since then, Satan's evil spirits have been germinating down through time so as to take hold of humanity through this spiritual invasion.

When the nature of Satan is sown and grown into man, the result is madness; which is what we see around us in the world today. The Bible shows explicitly that the degeneration of man can be brought to fruition if the mind is made to meditate upon the things of this world. Through the use of images in the media such as television, movies, music, video games, etc., the Devil is able to take the mind on a roller coaster ride into the spirit world. Over time, this will corrupt the very fabric of human thought. When this demonic onslaught is completed, the mind is left perverted and the soul is destroyed until finally it ends in the state of reprobation (Romans 1:20-32). The reprobate mind is one that is cast away and decadent; it longs for that which is perverse and totally destitute.

Friends, this consistent exposure to the Devil's mind and spirits turns man into the state of an animal. The Bible calls this corruption the mark of the Beast, where man himself has become a beast (Ecclesiastes 3:18; Revelation 19:20). What is Satan's goal? To prepare the world to receive his appointed king as the ruler over humanity: the Antichrist (Revelation 13:3, 17:13). However, the success of Satan's mission is contingent upon keeping humanity ignorant of his devices (2 Corinthians 2:11).

The Woman's Seed & The Serpent's Seed

Genesis 3:14-16
And the Lord God said unto the serpent, Because thou hast done this, thou art cursed above all cattle, and above every beast of the field; upon thy belly shalt thou go, and dust shalt thou eat all the days of thy life: and I will put enmity between thee and the woman, and between thy seed and her seed; it shall bruise thy head, and thou shalt bruise his heel. Unto the woman he said, I will greatly multiply thy sorrow and thy conception; in sorrow thou shalt bring forth children; and thy desire shall be to thy husband, and he shall rule over thee.

Notice that God was careful not to place enmity between the seed of the *man* and the seed of the serpent. Rather, God makes the distinction between the *woman's* seed and the serpent's seed. On the surface, this seems very unusual because women do not carry seed. It is the man who carries the seed while the woman supplies the egg which the seed fertilizes. However, God is making a prophetic statement here in reference to His Son Jesus Christ and the satanic seed that will always be Jesus' enemy.

Jesus was not born from the seed of a man, but of a woman because Mary bore Jesus without insemination from a man. In fulfillment of this prophecy, Satan bruised the heel of Jesus Christ (the woman's seed) on the cross. Yet on that same cross, Jesus dealt a death blow to the head of Satan's mutation of life, ending the rebellion and agony caused by Adam and Eve turning away from God.

In Genesis, God brings to life a creation made in His image and establishes mankind as sub-rulers over the earth. We also see Satan sowing seeds to bring about the genesis of *another* nature, one that corrupts Adam and Eve, leading them into rebellion against God. At that time, Adam and Eve housed **two natures** - the nature that came from God with a God-conscious mind and the nature that came from the Devil with a propensity towards sin. These contrary kingdoms present an antagonistic pull within man on the inside.

Those of you who have been born again of God's Spirit recognize that there are two natures warring for control within you (Romans 7:18-25). You have been born from above in your spirit, but at the same time there is a contrary nature in your flesh which still wants to rebel and operate outside of God's kingdom. The Adamic nature still wants to do what it desires, without God's input. This produces a tremendous internal struggle for control of your very being. The kingdom which wins in the end determines your eternal destiny. You can spend it in Heaven with God forever or be cast into Hell with Satan, his angels, and his Anti-Christ forever.

This is why this book has been written. In a day when the Gospel has been so polluted and convoluted, people desperately need to know what it *truly* means to be saved. The Organic Gospel has been written to make plain **God's plan for redemption** along with an analysis of this rebellious kingdom which stands up against it. To understand the magnitude of this struggle, one has only to look at the death of Jesus Christ on the cross.

Why did it take such a brutal, dramatic butchering of Jesus Christ in order to release us from Satan's captivity? Because Satan had organically grown *his nature* into the very fabric of mankind. Only by the death of that nature could we be released from the emotional, mental, and spiritual strongholds resulting from that captivity. Jesus put an end to the *organically* grown nature of Satan in man (the old/fallen man) so that the *organically* grown nature of Christ might take hold of us.

> *2 Peter 1:4*
> *Whereby are given unto us exceeding great and precious*
> *promises: that by these ye might be partakers of the divine*
> *nature, having escaped the corruption that is in the world*
> *through lust.*

Friends, make no mistake about it. We must reevaluate our conception of salvation, including what we have been taught through the years by religion. Religion has said that salvation is a gift from God - *unconditionally* given and maintained by Him - through a *one-time* confession of faith. I beg to differ.

Salvation is organically grown out of a human being. It is conceived in your spirit where it gestates and grows into your soul until it finally consumes your mortal body, resulting in evidence of your salvation. This is the process whereby God takes back the vessel He created by growing the nature of His Son Jesus Christ in us to **displace** the yokes of the Satanic seed planted long ago.

Remember, Adam and Eve are the parents of *all* humanity. They represented all mankind when they fell, opening the door to the satanic nature that has since grown into the very fabric of all men (Romans 5:12-19). Contrarily, the end time church is empowered by God to bring forth the manifestation of what was accomplished by Jesus many years ago: a resurrected life which has been fully released from its captivity to the Satanic nature. Once this occurs, Jesus will be revealed to the world as never before (John 14:12).

In order to be a part of this end-time move of God, you must understand the battle between these two natures. It is a dichotomy portrayed repeatedly in the Scriptures: Ishmael and Isaac; Esau and Jacob; Saul and David; Ahab and Elijah; the first Adam created in the Garden of Eden and the second Adam conceived in Mary's womb by the power of the Holy Spirit. Only those who understand the *magnitude* of this struggle will overcome that old, fallen nature. These individuals will be endowed with power by God to release captives from Satan's prison, taking the Gospel of the Kingdom around the world one last time before the end of this age comes (Daniel 11:32).

Just one question remains: *Are you willing to receive the engrafted word which is able to save your soul? Are you willing to endure with patience as the organic gospel grows **out of you** to reveal **Christ in you** - the hope of glory?*

It is time for the manifestation of the sons of God - those conceived by the Spirit, gestated from the spirit through the soul, and finally revealed as an end-time Body of Christ. These will be raised up by God in these last days to destroy the works of the Devil (Romans 8:19).

If not you, then who? If not now, then when? Will you answer the call?

This page intentionally left blank.

Chapter 2 - The Two Are Contrary One to the Other

The Flesh Lusts Against the Spirit

Genesis 4:1-15
And Adam knew Eve his wife; and she conceived, and bare Cain, and said, I have gotten a man from the Lord. And she again bare his brother Abel. And Abel was a keeper of sheep, but Cain was a tiller of the ground. And in process of time it came to pass, that Cain brought of the fruit of the ground an offering unto the Lord. And Abel, he also brought of the firstlings of his flock and of the fat thereof. And the Lord had respect unto Abel and to his offering: but unto Cain and to his offering he had not respect. And Cain was very wroth, and his countenance fell. And the Lord said unto Cain, Why art thou wroth? And why is thy countenance fallen? If thou doest well, shalt thou not be accepted? And if thou doest not well, sin lieth at the door. And unto thee shall be his desire, and thou shalt rule over him. And Cain talked with Abel his brother: and it came to pass, when they were in the field, that Cain rose up against Abel his brother, and slew him. And the Lord said unto Cain, Where is Abel thy brother? And he said, I know not: Am I my brother's keeper? And he said, What hast thou done? The voice of thy brother's blood crieth unto me from the ground. And now art thou cursed from the earth, which hath opened her mouth to receive thy brother's blood from thy hand; when thou tillest the ground, it shall not henceforth yield unto thee her strength; a fugitive and a vagabond shalt thou be in the earth. And Cain said unto the Lord, My punishment is greater than I can bear. Behold, thou hast driven me out this day from the face of the earth; and from thy face shall I be hid; and I shall be a fugitive and a vagabond in the earth; and it shall come to pass, that every one that findeth me shall slay me. And the Lord said unto him, Therefore whosoever slayeth Cain, vengeance shall be taken on him sevenfold. And the Lord set a mark upon Cain, lest any finding him should kill him.

The struggle between the two natures within Adam and Eve after the fall is embodied in their first two sons, Cain and Abel. A picture is painted of two different kinds of sons: one in submission to God and the other in rebellion against Him. Abel had a spirit of obedience, sacrificing what God commanded (Hebrews 11:4). Cain was full of pride, giving to God what was right in his own eyes. By nature, the rebellious son hated the obedient son, for the two are diametrically opposed to each other (Galatians 4:29). The spiritual seed reflected in Abel produces a martyr. The spiritual seed reflected in Cain produces a murderer. As it was then, so it is now.

The Bible is full of martyrdom and murder. Usually the one representing God is the one who's hated, ostracized, and martyred. Such are looked upon as outsiders and castaways by the world. In contrast, those coming from Cain's murderous seed are viewed as good world citizens, being obedient to the rules of the fallen empire. Such is the result of the genetic seed that came from God to make man in His image, which Satan corrupted to reflect his own image. These two lineages are plainly seen down through time with the defiled seed always at odds with the saints of God.

Obedient and disobedient people cannot walk together because the obedient one is a constant reminder that the rebellious person is not accepted by God. This is how Cain felt about Abel. When Cain saw Abel, he was confronted by the fact that his offering had been rejected. Abel's very existence reminded Cain that he was outside of God's Kingdom because he had offered an illegitimate sacrifice. Because of sin, a sacrifice must be made before man can enter into God's presence and God only receives the sacrifices **He** ordains; all else is strange fire (Leviticus 10:1-2; Numbers 26:61; Hebrews 9:20-23).

This is why Jesus Christ is the only way to the Father (John 14:6). He is the "*door*" which has been given as the access route (John 10:1-15). Our standing with God is not determined by what we decide is right, neither is it based upon what we deem necessary to receive God's forgiveness. God chooses the sacrifice and sets the parameters whereby we can fellowship with Him.

It makes no difference what religion you follow - Hinduism, Buddhism, Taoism, Islam, Roman Catholicism, Jehovah's Witnesses, Moonies, Mormons, etc. All religions which deny Jesus Christ as **the** sacrificial offering for sin prevent their adherents from being reconciled with God. Unless you accept Jesus Christ as the Lamb of God - and present yourself to Him so that your nature is methodically changed into *His nature* - you cannot be received in Heaven. The sons of God are only those who have been born of God, gestated by God, and manifested as His sons.

This is the sum of the struggle here on Earth. There is nothing a human being can do to make himself acceptable to God (Isaiah 64:6). You must come to God totally trusting the work performed by His Son Jesus Christ on a cross 2000 years ago to escape the damnation of the world to come. It's all about obedience to God and receiving the sin offering that He provided. God has provided a way of escape for us. Any other attempt to reach God will leave you rejected and damned because of your stubborn refusal to accept the way of escape that He has already designated.

Abel, an obedient servant who was murdered as a martyr, stands as a sign for all who would live godly in these last days (2 Timothy 3:12). He shows us the magnitude of hatred projected towards obedient children of God by those who refuse to obey Him. When you examine that struggle, you realize that the same combative attitude exists now all around the world.

Separating the Wheat from the Tares

The world is becoming increasingly more antagonistic towards Christians - not religious people, but truly born again Christians. The two are not the same.

Religious people are works-oriented; they focus on external performance such as going to church, reading their bibles, singing in choirs, and listening to sermons as if these religious activities are the *standard* and *sum* of the Christian experience. Religion itself is designed to keep you bound to the world by convincing you that adherence to its rituals makes you acceptable to God (Matthew 23:27-28).

A Christian on the other hand is focused on spiritual transformation (an inner work wrought by God). Having been regenerated to bear the image of Christ, they naturally sanctify themselves from the world so that His nature can germinate and grow without contamination.

> *1 John 2:15-17*
> *Love not the world, neither the things that are in the world. If any man love the world, the love of the Father is not in him. For all that is in the world, the lust of the flesh, and the lust of the eyes, and the pride of life, is not of the Father, but is of the world.*

The world's ideologies and perversions seek to choke off the life of Christ within. That is why there can be no compromise. Christ must be formed within us at the expense of everything else; it is all about nurturing organic growth. Just as a pregnant woman protects the life she carries so that she can bring it to full term, a born again believer sanctifies the life of Christ within so that His nature can show forth as evidence that we are children of God.

Brothers and sisters, it is time for us to realize that **radical** sanctification is necessary to produce Christ's nature within us. We must forsake all so that the nature of Christ takes hold, allowing us to produce spiritual fruit. Against such there is no law. There is no law for having to do the gymnastics of church life. Neither is there a law for having to perform to the standards of the pastor, deacons, or elders. Instead, you will serve God out of a pure heart *by nature*. This is God's objective as He organically grows Himself in His people.

The kingdom of God and Satan's kingdom war against each other because both spiritual entities are projected into the natural environment through yielded vessels; vessels whose inner most beings have been reformatted to reflect that particular nature. The more you sanctify yourself unto God, the more you become a house for God. The more you commit yourself to indulge in evil, the more you become a house for the Devil. It is not hard to understand. Just look around and you will see these two kingdoms manifesting through people's personalities.

The life of your inner "self" can be either good or evil based upon the spirit to whom you submit (Romans 6:16). Self can be *denied* so that God lives through you or self can be *gratified* so that Satan projects himself through you. The more selfless you are in sacrificing yourself over to God, the more His kingdom will grow organically in you to show forth His righteousness and love to others. The more selfish you are, the more Satan's kingdom will manifest out of you to show his pride, destruction, seduction, and lust. Selflessness and selfishness - two diametrically opposed forces - are both reflected through human beings as a testimony to which god is being served, the God of Heaven or the god of this world.

Remember that the human body is nothing more than a tabernacle; a place for spirits to live and show forth their personalities. As you look at your face in the mirror, you are not viewing the essence of who you are; only the body in which you live. You are a spirit who lives in a physical body and has a soul.

One of the hardest things for people to realize is the fact they are not their biological bodies. Whether male or female, you are not your body. The body returns back to dust while your spirit lives on eternally. In order to understand how organic growth occurs, you must know that your physical body is nothing more than a point of contact for the spirit world to show itself through on the physical plane.

Except A Seed Die

As you reformat your mind, soul, and character to conform to the mind of God, you begin to reflect His character by nature and not through effort. In dying to everything you were in the flesh, God's nature will take hold of you and empower you to live the Christian life. Conversely, Satan desires you to forsake self-denial and gratify yourself with a hedonistic lifestyle as witnessed by appetites being out of control. He says, *"Eat all you want! Have all the sex you like! Drink all the beer in the keg! Fill your mind with pornography, filth, and perversion. Live it up as you like! Have a good time! Eat, drink, and be merry for tomorrow we die and all we have is this life to enjoy!"* Satan deceives you into thinking that this world (including your life *in* this world) is the sum of your existence. Therefore, you remain controllable by him as you put all your effort into maintaining the here and now; the realm he controls as the god of this world.

This may be a shock for some, but God is **not** trying to save the world. He has already determined that this present world will not go on forever. God's mission is to destroy this world so that He can establish a new Heaven and Earth (Hebrews 1:10-12; Revelation 21:1). Where does that leave you if you have spent your whole life storing up treasures in this earthly realm (Matthew 6:19-21; 1 Timothy 6:17-19)? When God establishes His Kingdom on the earth, righteousness and peace will be the norm and the filth of this present world will be cast aside.

> *2 Peter 3:10-14*
> *But the day of the Lord will come as a thief in the night; in the which the heavens shall pass away with a great noise, and the elements shall melt with fervent heat, the earth also and the works that are therein shall be burned up. Seeing then that all these things shall be dissolved, what manner of persons ought ye to be in all holy conversation and godliness, looking for and hasting unto the coming of the day of God, wherein the heavens being on fire shall be dissolved, and the elements shall melt with fervent heat? Nevertheless we, according to his promise, look for new heavens and a new earth, wherein dwelleth righteousness. Wherefore, beloved, seeing that ye look for such things, be diligent that ye may be found of him in peace, without spot, and blameless.*

Don't fall for what some groups like the Jehovah's Witnesses proclaim when they say that this world will last forever. The word of God will steer you clear of *any* delusion. This Heaven and Earth are passing away. They will be burned up, dissolved, and replaced by a new Heaven and Earth wherein dwells righteousness. God is bringing this whole arena to a climax. He is going to fold up time and space so that eternity consumes it away. The Devil fights against the righteous kingdom of God because he knows that the end of this world means the end of his rule. As a result, anyone who seeks to have the kingdom of God manifest within them becomes the Devil's enemy.

Understand this: the Devil doesn't want this world to end so he gets those who serve him to love this present, evil world and make it their all. Thereby you can know that any message which attempts to get you to focus on this world is Satanic (Colossians 3:2). It is a snare of the enemy to prevent you from escaping his control. God's plan is not for you to have your "best life now", but to exchange your soulish life for a spiritual life so as to receive the gift of eternal life with Him. The only battle we face in this world is the inner war between good and evil, righteousness and unrighteousness, obedience and rebellion. The question to consider is:, "Will we let that satanic, Adamic seed die so that Christ may live?" (John 12:24).

If you allow Christ - the obedient Son - to take hold of you, then the rebellious seed from the Devil's nature will fight you. That is just the way it is. It is the lot you have drawn as part of your inheritance. As we enter into this end-time struggle, somebody has to resign himself to engage in this inner war so that the nature of Jesus Christ can come to maturity. Your own flesh, mind, and emotions will war against you. Everything in you that has been programmed to be like the Devil will stand against you. Remember, the flesh wars against the spirit; the spirit wars against the flesh; the two are contrary one to another so that you do not do those things that you would do (Galatians 5:17). There is a fallen nature in you that is fighting against you. However, through the willful act of obedience and discipline under the word of God, you can beat down the flesh. Such is what must happen if you want Christ to grow out of you and manifest **Him** as the answer for all of mankind's problems.

Man does not need psychological evaluations, political spin, or pundits' points of view. We have listened to all the theorists regarding what is wrong. We have the ways man has said things should be done, and none have worked. Jesus Christ *in you* is the only answer for man (Colossians 1:27). There is no other. Yet, because man is intent on finding an answer apart from Christ, talk show hosts make millions of dollars discussing man's problems all day when there is really no discussion to be had. You and I must manifest Christ out of us in order to be made free. You shall know the Truth and the Truth shall make you free (John 8:32). Jesus said in John 14:6, "*I am the way, the truth, and the life; no man comes to the Father but by me.*" If you are looking for any other answer then you will be deceived.

In these last of the last days, friends, you had better seek out, pursue, and bathe yourself in the word of God. Not as a work or as something to perform for God. Rather, in order to feed the seed sown in you. If Christ has been sown in you, then He has to live at your expense through self-denial. Such is the way of escape. This is how you come out of Egypt (the world) and cross over into Canaan (the Promised Land). The Gospel must be organically grown out of us, taking hold of our minds so as to liberate us from the Devil's clutches.

Remember, you were born in sin and shaped in iniquity (Psalm 51:5). You were *by nature* children of wrath; rebellious and disobedient possessing the nature of the Devil within (Ephesians 2:3). That is why you sinned. No one sins because they have engaged in deep analysis before making a conscious choice to do so. People sin because they possess the nature of a sinner. Sin is not primarily *what you do*; it is *who you are*. By nature fish swim, dogs bark, and birds fly. Your nature dictates your actions, not vice versa. For example, no matter how much I swim, bark, or flap my arms, it will never make me a fish, a dog, or a bird. Likewise, no matter how much I try to do good, my nature remains that of a sinner outside of Christ. My sin was just the evidence or fruit of the nature I possessed. Yet, religion will have you putting on a happy face as you try and pretend to be other than what you truly are.

My son used to attend a school based upon Baptist doctrine [I'm very careful not to call religious schools "Christian" school because I find very few to be.]. One day, a 4th grade classmate told him a lie. Since my son has been taught that lying is a sin, he called his classmate a liar and stated that continuing to lie would send you to Hell. The Supervisor of that school then sent me a note stating that my son was condemning another student and needed to learn to use God's word in love without condemnation.

When speaking the word of God in love means that we have to deny the truths of the Scripture, we can know for certain that we are seeing a manifestation of end-time delusions. When being loving means not telling me that I am doing wrong, you are being prepared to receive the Anti-Christ as your god. I told my son he was absolutely right in what he said, but that a religious environment can never receive the truth. This is why we have to use wisdom when dealing with the world's systems. The tragic part is my son's classmate was being taught that it is okay to lie. You can sin and nobody will say a thing because they don't want to condemn you and make you feel bad. This is how perverted society has become.

The fact of the matter is we cannot *use* the word of God at all; the word of God *uses* you and me. God uses man; man cannot use God. The word of God is not data coming out of the Bible, but a living being who houses Himself in you and me. The realm of religion has been intruded upon by Satan and his perversion is now propagated as truth. According to his presentation, Christianity is the equivalent of tolerance of sin (called diversity), not judging anything, and letting everybody do their own thing. To the religious mind, it is compassionate not to speak against sin. Yet God never downgrades His truths about sin nor His penalty for it.

Make no mistake about it; God will damn a sinner's soul to Hell forever because the nature of sin is against Him. Sin must be dealt with by receiving the penalty for sin: Jesus Christ's death on the cross. Remember, Jesus did not die *for* you. Jesus **took you to the cross** to mortify that sin nature and kill it there. The Apostle Paul plainly states, *"I am crucified with Christ; nevertheless I live; yet not I, but Christ liveth within me."* (Galatians 2:20). You don't go to the cross to be free from sin as some would say; you must go *through* the cross. This is the missing element in Christianity - the cross being self-applied as opposed to simply being a religious relic upon which to look.

The cross of Jesus Christ is where the Divine and the Satanic natures come into complete contrast and conflict. One is left on the cross dead while the other comes out of the tomb resurrected three days later. The only way to get the new nature is to kill the old one; one must die for the other to live (Luke 9:24). I am emphasizing this so that you will understand it clearly. **If you do not crucify the flesh, the flesh *will* crucify Christ in you.** If you do not mortify the members of the sinful nature, that sinful nature and its lust for the world will disallow the life of Christ being formed in you.

The struggle deep down in the human character is the struggle for control of the human soul. The old man will struggle for life against the inner invasion coming from Christ as Jesus implants Himself within you supernaturally through the new birth. As the life of Christ germinates from your spirit and into your soul, the divine nature will begin to take over your mind, will, emotions, and thoughts until finally a new man manifests out of you to a sin-sick, dying world (Ephesians 4:20-24; Colossians 3:8-10). As evidence that Christ's nature has not only been conceived, but brought to maturity within you, there will be a confirmation of signs, wonders, and power in your life. Remember, the Apostle Paul says that he did not come into town with enticing words of man's wisdom, but he came with the demonstration of the Spirit of God and power, so that faith would not stand on the words of men and their wisdom but on the power of God (1 Corinthians 2:4-5).

Struggles that take place in the human personality are all based on the two natures vying for preeminence. Unsaved persons are yielded to the flesh and the dictates of their master Satan. They are basically slaves, carrying out the will of an unseen agent that drives and compels them through addictions to the things of this world (2 Timothy 2:26). When a person is born again, his spirit is brought back to life as God initiates an inner war to take back that vessel from the Devil. In Luke 21:19, Jesus states, *"In your patience, possess ye your souls."* In your patience, **take possession** of your own soul. Take back the arena that the Devil has been influencing your whole life. Friend, every Christian, must engage in that inner struggle to take back ground from the Devil.

A lot of you have been taught that Christians cannot have demon spirits, and I agree with you. Christians cannot have demon spirits because a Christian is a spirit and your spirit has been born again. However, the realm of your soul and your physical body must be taken from the auspices of the Devil by force (Matthew 11:12). Your spirit man - clad in spiritual armor and girded with power by the word of God - orchestrates a warfare to take possession of your soul (Ephesians 6:13-17). Instead of being ruled by the inordinate passions of the soul, your spirit will seek to establish Godly order within you. This will bring your soul and body in subjection to itself as your spirit receives from, and submits to, the Spirit of God. This results in demons being cast out and the flesh being mortified as Jesus indeed becomes Lord over your life (1 Corinthians 12:3). Such is the struggle you experience in your members.

Don't listen to those who are unlearned and unstable in the ways of righteousness (2 Peter 3:14-18). You must not only be saved and converted by the Holy Ghost, but you need to be baptized and continually filled with the Holy Ghost. That is when the war takes place friend. God will save you and baptize you, but **you must deny yourself** and prosecute a war to be filled. Once filled, the Apostle tells us that he had to stay under his body to avoid becoming a castaway after preaching the gospel. It is not enough to be filled with the Spirit at one time, but you must bring your body into subjection so as to stay filled (1 Corinthians 9:27).

> *Acts 1:7-8*
> *And he said unto them, It is not for you to know the times or the seasons, which the Father hath put in his own power. But ye shall receive power after that the Holy Ghost is come upon you: and ye shall be witnesses unto me both in Jerusalem, and in all Judaea, and in Samaria, and unto the uttermost part of the earth.*

The word *"witness"* is the Greek word for a martyr, a sacrifice. A life must be sacrificed to God for Him to use you as His witness (Romans

12:1). These disciples became witnesses unto God, starting in Jerusalem, moving to Judaea, into Samaria, and then the whole Earth. This is a picture of organic growth. It starts in one place and grows from there, multiplying until it fills the entire earth.

In order to produce a sacrifice through which God can manifest His perfect will, there will have to be a struggle. One life has to die for the other to live. The Christian life is one of **war** as two natures which began in the Garden of Eden vie for preeminence. The nature of Cain has its citadel setup in the soul, while the nature of Abel resides in your spirit. Both are organically grown out of the very fabric of your being, defining not only who, but whose you are; either a son of God or a son of the serpent. Make no mistake about it, we are headed for a final conflict between these two natures, as evidenced by growing reports of homosexuality, feminism, and ethnic unrest in the media. Remember, the serpent seed is at enmity with the seed of the woman (Christ in you).

In these last days, you must evaluate - not merely what you do, where you go, the church to which you belong, or the doctrine you believe - but what you are? What really has control over you? In a pressurized situation, when the blows of the world come down upon you, your true nature will automatically take over. Two things stand sure in these last days: organic growth is an individual affair and what you are *organically* cannot be faked.

A lot of you reading this book know deep within that you have been faking Christianity. You have been trying to look, act, and speak like what you believe a Christian should be, but you have only experienced frustration. You personally know the agony of trying to be what you have not been organically grown to be because the life of Christ is not within. Do not continue to delude yourself because the times around us are intensifying. Under pressure, you will forsake the play acting and your real nature will take control. Examine what Jesus says about the deception that's coming upon millions in these last days.

> *Matthew 7:21-23*
> *Not every one that saith unto me, Lord, Lord, shall enter into the kingdom of heaven; but he that doeth the will of my Father which is in heaven. Many will say to me in that day, Lord, Lord, have we not prophesied in thy name? And in thy name have cast out devils? And in thy name done many wonderful works? And then will I profess unto them, I never knew you: depart from me, ye that work iniquity.*

The Two Are Contrary One to the Other

What chilling words. The people are crying, *"Lord we've done all these wonderful works in Your name - casting out devils, prophesying..."* Yet Jesus comes back with a startling and terrifying response, *"I never knew you."* Notice that He did not say He once knew you and has since forgotten you. Why does Jesus say this? Because they were never made one with Christ. The word "knew" in this text is the same word referencing a man knowing his wife through consummation of the marriage. It refers to a type of communion where two become one. Yet these individuals never had the nature of Christ imparted to them by being truly born again. They chose religious works (outward performance) over the organic nature of Christ (an inner work). The greatest sin of all in the church world is the sin of hypocrisy.

As a believer in Christ Jesus, you are to be in intimate communion with Him as a Bride is with her Groom. This spiritual intercourse with Jesus is the means by which you receive the engrafted word which is able to save your soul (James 1:21). The Word gestating inside of you results in a manifestation of sonship coming out from you as Christ's nature is formed within. This transformation into the image of Christ testifies to the sealing of your covenant with God and qualifies you for the life to come in Heaven (Romans 8:28-29; 2 Corinthians 3:18). Remember, Jesus said that the kingdom of Heaven does not come with observation, but is within you. The kingdom of God is birthed in you *organically*.

When told the truth, the vast majority of church people respond in anger, negativity, and hatred because their nature has not been organically changed. Only when that nature has been offered up so that the nature of Jesus Christ takes hold can you be a witness for Christ; it comes at the expense of that old man.

The power struggle between these two natures goes on, yet the questions remain. Where are you in this struggle? Whose side are you on? Do these words cause you to squirm in your seat and fume in anger? If they do, beware that you be not destroyed, deceiving yourself. The lineage of Cain will murder the end-time saints for the same reasons that Cain murdered Abel: they stand rejected by God, not having offered a legitimate sacrifice to Him. The sacrifice required of us is the sacrifice of our very lives.

> *Revelation 12:11*
> *And they overcame him by the blood of the Lamb, and by the word of their testimony; and they loved not their lives unto the death.*

The true Gospel message is too austere, too disciplined, and too other-worldly for those who love this world (including their lives in this world).

The culmination of the struggle will be between saints of God (bearing the image of Christ) and the sodomites of Babylon (who bear the image of Satan). Carefully evaluate it, friends, and decide to which side you will commit, for the time is at hand.

Chapter 3 - Seed Sown Amongst the Thorns

Caught in the Weeds

Deuteronomy 22:9
Thou shalt not sow thy vineyard with divers seeds: lest the
fruit of thy seed which thou hast sown, and the fruit of thy
vineyard, be defiled.

One of the most detestable things in God's eyes is to mix His seed with the seed of the serpent. Deuteronomy Chapter 22 warns that sowing your vineyard with diverse seeds will defile both the seed and the resulting fruit. Such is the snare in the present day Church. The works of the flesh have been mixed with the righteous seed of God's word, producing a kaleidoscope of confusion. The devil cannot destroy the Church from the outside, so his only hope is to mix himself <u>inside</u> the Church and weaken it from within. Satan makes inroads into the Church via a fifth column. The Encyclopedia Britannica describes a fifth column as follows:

"A military tactic where a clandestine group or faction of subversive agents attempt to undermine another's solidarity by any means at their disposal. A cardinal technique of the fifth column is the infiltration of sympathizers into the entire fabric of the entity under attack and, particularly, into positions of policy decision and defense. From such key posts, they can exploit fears by spreading rumours and misinformation, as well as by employing the more standard techniques of espionage and sabotage."

The Devil is a cunning creature, possessing a mind skilled in deception and illusion. Part of what makes him such a formidable foe is that he exploits the Church's ignorance of the spirit world. Since much of the Church remains carnal and ensnared by the things of this world, Satan is able to project his kingdom into the Church **spiritually**, and therefore largely undetected.

Make no mistake about it friends, you cannot fight a spiritual battle with carnal weapons. 2 Corinthians Chapter 10:4 states, *"the weapons of our warfare are not carnal; they are mighty through God by the pulling down of strongholds."* Spiritual weapons must be launched to destroy a spiritual enemy; and for that to happen we must have spiritual eyes to see. As long as the Devil is able to continue mixing himself into the Church, we will remain disempowered and unable to stop his advancement.

The truth is that the hearts of many Christians are divided; they still love the world in some manner. Satan is able to use this idolatry to blind them to his spiritual attacks as he weaves his way into the soul. Whether it is the government, media, entertainment, religion, psychology, or some other worldly system, Christians are feeding on the wisdom of this world. As a result, the cares of this world choke off the seed sown leading many to only mimic the life we ought to have in Christ by turning to good works.

While God has prepared His people to perform good works - building homes for the needy, feeding the hungry, clothing the naked, etc. - these alone are poor substitutes for the actual life of Jesus Christ living within us. These are not the foundation upon which we stand. If good works alone are the standard of righteousness, then there is no difference between the Christian and anyone else. Satanists can build homes. Muslims can build youth centers. Mormons can take your grandmother out to buy groceries. While these are all good things to do, they are all *temporal* and do not impact Satan nor destroy his kingdom. The Scriptures say that the primary reason for which Jesus was manifested in the flesh was to destroy the works of the devil (I John 3:8). Unless destroying every vestige of Satan's kingdom is our goal, then we are not focused on doing the Father's business.

> *Luke 4:18-19*
> *"The Spirit of the Lord is upon me, because he hath anointed me to preach the gospel to the poor; he hath sent me to heal the brokenhearted, to preach deliverance to the captives, and recovering of sight to the blind, to set at liberty them that are bruised, to preach the acceptable year of the Lord."*

Jesus gave specifics about the mission given to Him by the Father. He was appointed and anointed to preach the gospel to the poor, to heal brokenhearted people, to preach deliverance to people who are imprisoned, to recover sight for blind people, to free those who were wounded, and to preach the acceptable year of the Lord. Jesus was on a mission to rend captive people out of the hands of their captor, Satan.

While the Body of Christ should be dedicated to that same mission, many Christians are now caught up in church bazaars, music concerts, pastor appreciation dinners, Tom Thumb weddings, and other functions. We have come to the point where fellowship and church service has become a ritual and an idolatrous festival for many. Since the wrong seed has been mixed into the church, the mission, focus, and impetus of the Gospel is largely lost.

Seed Sown Amongst the Thorns

When you mix the fallen Adamic nature (which is the seed of Satan) with the righteous seed of Christ, you get a subtle **neutralization** of the power of God. The Gospel becomes Earth-centered instead of Heavenly-driven. Christians who were once on fire for God become complacent, lackadaisical, lethargic, laid back, and comfortable because their desires begin to focus on this present world. They lose the zeal and the propulsion necessary to reach the lost and to lead people out of darkness and into the light. Without a vision, God's people will perish (Proverbs 29:18). If there is no deep-rooted desire for Heaven within the heart of a Christian, then the desire to see Christ living in us will be lost. This is why Deuteronomy says, *"Don't mix the seed sown in the field."* Don't dilute and diffuse what God is doing by mixing in seed of another source.

Satan mixes into the church by transforming himself into a nice guy or as the Scriptures say, *"an angel of light"* (2 Corinthians 11:14). He comes across as cordial, respectable, kind, and so very humane that one in a million couldn't detect him. Satan has become so deft at emulating man and appealing to what pampers man's flesh that he appears as a likeable, charismatic personality to the natural man. This draw of charisma has been the perfect setup for the current age of the megachurch where thousands join a congregation based upon the personality of the preacher. The truly deceptive part is that the sheer number of people involved makes you feel like you have found the truth. My friend, numbers do not dictate truth nor do they dictate reality. We all know that swelling is a sure sign of infection. Truth is a person - Jesus Christ - who must be known in the inner man through obedience, discipline, fellowship and communion spent with Him.

Maybe you have gone for the devil's make-believe presentation of the Gospel because it appeases your innermost need to belong and be accepted. It appeals to your desire to live in comfort and not to be put under duress. However, I am here to tell you that the Gospel of Jesus Christ *will* place you under duress and move you out of your comfort zone. It will take you into a realm for which you have not bargained because it propagates and compels you into **war**.

Jesus said that His kingdom was not of this world. Had it been of this world, His subjects would have fought for Him (John 18:36). This should let us know that trying to belong to this world makes us unacceptable to God. Knowing that God must reject those who love the world, Satan has spent billions of dollars to deeply entrench the world into the church. He has so mixed the two that the world is in the church and the church is in the world. Friends, it is right for the church to be in the world, but for the world to be in the church equates to damnation.

The Church - God's *ekklesia* - is a group of "called out" ones who have been set apart by God for His purposes. He desires to mold us into His image so that He can fill us with the eternal power of the Holy Ghost as living witnesses of Him. There is no other way to be reconciled to God except to be sanctified unto holiness.

2 Corinthians 6:14-18
Be ye not unequally yoked together with unbelievers: for what fellowship hath righteousness with unrighteousness? And what communion hath light with darkness? And what concord hath Christ with Belial? Or what part hath he that believeth with an infidel? And what agreement hath the temple of God with idols? For ye are the temple of the living God; as God hath said, I will dwell in them, and walk in them; and I will be their God, and they shall be my people. Wherefore come out from among them, and be ye separate, saith the Lord, and touch not the unclean thing; and I will receive you, and will be a Father unto you, and ye shall be my sons and daughters, saith the Lord Almighty.

Brothers and sisters, we must come out from amongst them. We must separate from the Devil's vexations which are sent to stop the formation of Jesus Christ within us. Only when the word of God is sown in our spirit and the nature of Christ is grown out into the soul do we become living witnesses as He manifests through our physical bodies. That transformation in itself testifies to the world that God is not dead, but alive!

The commands that Jesus gave in Mark 16:17-20 are still valid for our generation: saving souls, casting out devils, raising the dead, healing the sick, opening blind eyes, and doing the same works that Jesus did when He walked on the earth over 2000 years ago. We must cast out the perverted seed from Satan so that the righteous seed from Christ can shine forth in order for God to be seen in this generation.

In the world, these two kingdoms grow simultaneously together. Jesus says to allow the tares and wheat to grow up together (Matthew 13:30). Tares sown by the Devil are used by the false religious system to choke off the life of God within His children in an effort to stop their growth and maturity in Christ. Only those who are chosen and who have remained faithful will go on to perfection in spite of Satan's schemes. At that point, there is a separation as the tares are bundled together by the angels to be burned and God's children shine forth like the morning to demonstrate His power.

Friend, do not allow the Devil to strangle off your spiritual life by sowing mingled seed into your soul. It will cause defects in your new birth when Christ seeks to be formed in you. These are tumultuous & chaotic times. You must focus your mind on the word of God to stay steadfast and immovable, always abounding in the grace of Jesus Christ (1 Corinthians 15:58).

Let us look at some examples of how the Devil has mingled his perverse seed in with the church. Use this as an opportunity to examine yourselves. Consider whether you have ingested that which perverts the fruit of God in your life and might even lead you to forsake Christ.

Defiled Fruit

The Gospel of Prosperity

> *2 Peter 2:1-22*
> *But there were false prophets also among the people, even as there shall be false teachers among you, who privily shall bring in damnable heresies, even denying the Lord that bought them, and bring upon themselves swift destruction. And many shall follow their pernicious ways; by reason of whom the way of truth shall be evil spoken of.* ***And through covetousness shall they with feigned words make merchandise of you****: whose judgment now of a long time lingereth not, and their damnation slumbereth not.*
>
> *For if God spared not the angels that sinned, but cast them down to hell, and delivered them into chains of darkness, to be reserved unto judgment; and spared not the old world, but saved Noah the eighth person, a preacher of righteousness, bringing in the flood upon the world of the ungodly; and turning the cities of Sodom and Gomorrha into ashes condemned them with an overthrow, making them an ensample unto those that after should live ungodly; and delivered just Lot, vexed with the filthy conversation of the wicked: (For that righteous man dwelling among them, in seeing and hearing, vexed his righteous soul from day to day with their unlawful deeds;) the Lord knoweth how to deliver the godly out of temptations, and to reserve the unjust unto the day of judgment to be punished: but chiefly them that walk after the flesh in the lust of uncleanness, and despise government. Presumptuous are they, self-willed,*

they are not afraid to speak evil of dignities. Whereas angels, which are greater in power and might, bring not railing accusation against them before the Lord. But these, as natural brute beasts, made to be taken and destroyed, speak evil of the things that they understand not; and shall utterly perish in their own corruption; and shall receive the reward of unrighteousness, as they that count it pleasure to riot in the day time.

*Spots they are and blemishes, sporting themselves with their own deceivings while they feast with you; having eyes full of adultery, and that cannot cease from sin; beguiling unstable souls: an heart they have exercised with covetous practices; cursed children: which have forsaken the right way, and are gone astray, following the way of Balaam the son of Bosor, who **loved the wages of unrighteousness**; but was rebuked for his iniquity: the dumb ass speaking with man's voice forbad the madness of the prophet.*

*These are wells without water, clouds that are carried with a tempest; to whom the mist of darkness is reserved for ever. For when they speak great swelling words of vanity, **they allure through the lusts of the flesh**, through much wantonness, those that were clean escaped from them who live in error. While they promise them liberty, they themselves are the servants of corruption: for of whom a man is overcome, of the same is he brought in bondage. For if after they have escaped the pollutions of the world through the knowledge of the Lord and Saviour Jesus Christ, they are again entangled therein, and overcome, the latter end is worse with them than the beginning. For it had been better for them not to have known the way of righteousness, than, after they have known it, to turn from the holy commandment delivered unto them. But it is happened unto them according to the true proverb, the dog is turned to his own vomit again; and the sow that was washed to her wallowing in the mire.*

In 2 Peter, Chapter 2, the Apostle Peter speaks of a particular delusion which was to come. He says that men would begin to seek church leaders who preach according to the lusts of their own flesh. This means that the most prominent snare to our development as sons of God could be *professing* Christians whose affections have turned back to the world and who desire to turn us back as well.

True to Peter's warning, a gospel of greed emerged in the late sixties as men such as Kenneth Hagin, Frederick Price, Charles Capps, Kenneth Copeland, and Granville "Oral" Roberts preached that Jesus came so that we could be rich. Faith, they claimed, is a force which can be used by us to acquire material wealth. Now, the generations of prosperity preachers which follow - Creflo Dollar, T. D. Jakes, Robert "Bob" Tilton, Eddie Long, Benny Hinn, Joyce Meyers, etc. - seem to have no shame. They arrogantly flaunt their greed and ill-gotten gain of tithes made possible through sorceries performed on the masses. They have, in essence, become modern day stars with this false gospel; flying around in Lear jets, driving Rolls Royces, and living in multi-million dollar homes with a seemingly insatiable appetite for more.

By bringing in damnable heresies - even denying the Lord who bought them - the truth is considered **evil** by their followers as these false preachers spew lies from pulpits all over the world. Twisting Scripture to support their perverted gospel, they seek to manipulate the minds of the masses and be worshipped as gods themselves. Those who are unlearned and untaught in the word of God flock to these places, seeking after the wealth, glamour & glitz they are promised for paying tithes to these false prophets. It is a shame to be deceived by a false prophet, but it's a **double shame** to pay them money to damn your soul to Hell forever.

It is not uncommon for these preachers to have spiritual (and sometimes physical) concubines in their congregations; both male and female. Rejected souls seeking acceptance become enamored with their personalities, hype, and Hollywood lifestyles. Far from being the favor of God, money flows like a river towards these deceivers because they are living off of the tithes brought into the whorehouses they have built. This is the power of Satan as he hides himself behind the pulpits.

Take heed and beware of the gospel of greed. Equating gain with godliness turns you away from the truth, causing you to fall into many hurtful snares of the Devil (1 Timothy 6:5, 9-10). There is a deceitfulness that comes from riches because it competes with, and can choke off, your growth in Christ (Mark 4:19). Yet many have bought into this delusion, including many reading this book. Mega-ministries and mega-stars dot the landscape as lying wonders, perpetrating a fraud on the masses. It is nothing less than a demonic scheme to draw people away from salvation and into the one thing that makes them the enemy of God: a love for the world (1 John 2:15-16; James 4:4). Caught in this deception, you will care more about your social standing and prominence in this world than about being in right relationship with Jesus Christ. The end result is that these preachers - and those who follow their pernicious or *damnable* ways - bring upon themselves destruction.

Yet, the most revealing aspect of this Scripture is found in verse 3 as Peter explains why this delusion attains such prominence: the people are bound by, and anchored to, covetousness. People gravitate to this fleshly gospel because it promises a monetary return from God based upon what they give. Therefore, men are able to build empires off of people's carnal lusts. What makes these prosperity lies so tragic is how they pervert the Gospel, turning it primarily into a tool for you to use to accomplish *your* will. With this mindset, you will take no thought for the actual purpose of the Gospel in establishing God's kingdom and having *His* will done through you.

Brothers and sisters, God's goal in saving you was not to make you financially rich. God saved you to **redeem** you from the clutches of sin: your body, soul, and spirit. Only when you have been set free can you have fellowship with Him, presenting yourself sacrificially to God to be filled with His Spirit. At that point, you will manifest to the world as a vessel of honor, showing forth the life of Jesus Christ to a dying world.

Make no mistake about it friend. When a preacher is promoting false doctrine, you had better believe there are nests of demons lurking in the shadows. Behind the religious veneer you will find a culture filled with adultery, fornication, perversion, homosexuality, lesbianism, pornography, and enough filth to warp your mind if God's Spirit is not anchoring your soul. The picture of prosperity being painted by these hucksters and shamans is only an illusion because God has already judged them. You will begin to see the dismantling of an empire built on fantasy and make-believe as their wickedness is revealed (Luke 8:17). Many will be left distraught and bewildered by the sudden demise of spiritual Babylon as these false prognosticators fall one by one (Revelation 18:8). Remember, Babylon is a culture that's intertwined with all worldly systems globally: government, economic, social, entertainment, religious, etc.

Wealth is an idol in the world and people worship those who have it because of covetousness. This greed is being used by the Devil to mesmerize those whose hearts still desire worldly success, allowing him to blind the minds of hundreds of millions of people. Make sure your soul is cleansed from this perversion and stay away from these wicked wizards of prosperity because God is about to judge that entire realm of Babylon. He warns us to come out from such places so that we do not partake of her sins and receive of her plagues. Don't be snared and enticed by the glitzy, glamorous world of the megachurch.

The Bible says, "...*broad is the way, that leadeth to destruction, and many there be which go in thereat,"* but conversely, *"strait is the gate, and narrow is the way, which leadeth unto life, and few there be that find it.* (Matthew 7:13-14)" By this we can know that the place where the majority flocks is most likely to be the place which leads to destruction and damnation. You do not become a partaker of the Gospel by simply being a member of the herd. Salvation is an individual affair where you come to intimately know Christ for yourself, resulting in His very nature and character being conceived in you. Only then can His life be manifested within you as a witness unto the world. The Gospel must be organically grown out of **you**! We must examine ourselves concerning our own desires to see what we are really after because the gospel of greed is alluring, mesmerizing, and pervasive. It promises you the world, but at the end of that road you'll find swift and sudden destruction.

Religious Denominationalism

> *James 1:26-27*
> *If any man among you seem to be religious, and bridleth not his tongue, but deceiveth his own heart, this man's religion is vain. Pure religion and undefiled before God and the Father is this, To visit the fatherless and widows in their affliction, and to keep himself unspotted from the world.*

One of the most powerful spirits released on Earth right now is the religious spirit. It anchors a man's soul to organizational membership as the sign-off on your salvation. Such is filthy and detestable to God because it is this type of structure which crucified Christ (Galatians 1:13-14; Revelation 2:6, 15). Make no mistake about it: religion hates God. It will by nature fight the organic development of Christ within you because it is built upon the idolatry of man. Yes, man may superficially accept God's truths by intellectually acknowledging its righteousness (called mental ascension), but there is never a heart change allowing him to obey God's commands. The best that the religions of the world can offer is to seek to make you socially acceptable to the world and a "nice person" in the eyes of your contemporaries.

Satan is the god that rules religion. His demonic forces have cultivated and grown religious systems so captivating that most people cannot understand the fact that they are lost even while sitting in these churches. These systems will have you convinced that you serve God, even while totally denying everything He says in His word. These sorceries are so powerful, they can convince a person that he is righteous and saved, while keeping him on the pathway to Hell. They impart to you a form of godliness, but deny the power needed to transform you into what you profess to be. Look closely at the Scriptures as Paul warns Timothy, a young preacher, about the pitfalls of religion:

> *2 Timothy 3:1-9:*
> *This know also, that in the last days perilous times shall come. For men shall be lovers of their own selves, covetous, boasters, proud, blasphemers, disobedient to parents, unthankful, unholy, without natural affection, trucebreakers, false accusers, incontinent, fierce, despisers of those that are good, traitors, heady, high-minded, lovers of pleasures more than lovers of God; having a form of godliness, but denying the power thereof: from such turn away. For of this sort are they which creep into houses, and lead captive silly women laden with sins, led away with divers lusts, ever learning, and never able to come to the knowledge of the truth. Now as Jannes and Jambres withstood Moses, so do these also resist the truth: men of corrupt minds, reprobate concerning the faith. But they shall proceed no further: for their folly shall be manifest unto all men, as theirs also was.*

Verse five states that the members of this organized, religious system **all** have a "*form*" of godliness, but they deny the power thereof. They appear godly on the outside - reciting religious phrases, attending church functions, carrying a Bible, giving offerings, etc. - but they have no ability to live out the life they profess to have obtained. They are not sanctified by God unto holiness because they still desire the things of this world in their hearts. As a result, the power of God does not rest upon them, testifying to the fact that they do not bear the life of Christ within. In the last days, man will be forced to make a choice between a relationship *with* God versus religious performance *about* God.

The Bible is plain that there is no room for debate or compromise: church membership and religious structures **cannot** save you. The confirmation that powers of darkness operate in and through the religious church world is the *absence* of God's power amongst the people. That power is being short-circuited by man's carnal nature. In fact, religion makes sure to feed this nature so as to keep man's affections on things in the earth instead of things above (Colossians 3:1-2). Religion centers around life on Earth while relationship with Jesus prepares you for a life in eternity with Him forever. This is the conflict, the contrast, the war in which we have enlisted: two natures vying for preeminence in our souls - the nature of fallen man versus the nature of Jesus Christ. God's people perish due to a lack of knowledge (Hosea 4:6). Being ignorant of the deceitful snares of religion will lead to your destruction in the end.

Religious structures such as Roman Catholicism, Mormonism, Jehovah's Witnesses, Hinduism, Buddhism, Taoism, Confucianism, Islam, Baptist, Methodist, Protestants, Reformers, etc. cannot replicate God's process of imparting life to you. No matter what brand you go by, they are all built by man and are unacceptable to Jesus Christ. Jesus is not looking for your name on a church membership roll as the confirmation that you belong to Him. He is looking for those who worship Him in spirit and in truth (John 4:23-24). Only those who love Jesus above all else will desire to be freed from the snares of this world, including the institutionalized structures set up by Satan to control the minds of men.

One of the most damnable sin makers on Earth is Calvinism. Their belief system is reflected in the acronym T.U.L.I.P. The "T" stands for total depravity. This not only represents that you cannot save yourself (which you cannot), but that you do not even have the God-given will to choose faith in the Savior. The "U" represents unconditional election, meaning that God chooses who will be saved and who will be damned arbitrarily, based on no condition other than His own Sovereign will. The "L" means limited atonement, which asserts that Jesus did not die for the sin of the world, but only for those whom God chose. "I" is irresistible grace, reinforcing their belief that humans do not have free will; you cannot choose to be saved and you cannot resist God's calling. Lastly, "P" is perseverance of the saints which states that, because God's election of you is not connected to any condition, you can never fall away. Once you are saved, you are always saved.

I am not picking on Calvinists here, but I want to illustrate how damnable heresies are. They are designed to blur the truths of God so that you wind up following after man. Many of these same errors permeate other denominations such as the Baptist church. You would have to be blind to read Hebrews Chapter 6 and not see that you can fall away from the faith. You can turn away after you have received the revelation of Christ so that you cannot be renewed again unto repentance. Why "*again*"? Because they had already been renewed previously. We are not saved in sin, but we are saved from sin. The definition of a saint is one who has been sanctified and separated *from* sin. These biblical distortions are why so many religious people are filled with pride; "I am a chosen one, and you are not." They often cannot receive the truth because their pride will not let them.

In speaking of the last days, Jesus said in Matthew 24:4, "*Take heed that no man deceive you!"* You have to come to the Lord lowly; crawling face down, begging for God to have mercy on your soul. Everyone in the Bible who received help from God threw themselves down face first and cried out, *"Lord be merciful unto me a sinner."* You must choose to **humble yourself** in order to receive Him and be received by Him; and that takes an act of your will (2 Chronicles 7:14, 34:27; James 4:10). This is what Calvinists disallow, because according to them, you have no free will. That is absolutely crazy - not to mention against the Scriptures - and you would have to be insane to believe it!

You see how they always name doctrines after man? Wesley, Calvin, Luther, etc. The Word of God - Jesus Christ - is who we follow, not man's teachings and interpretation. No Scripture is of private interpretation, but holy men spoke as they were moved upon by the Holy Ghost of God. The final arbiter of truth is the word of God (2 Peter 1:20).

Man was designed to be a creature of worship so that his spirit could fellowship with God. Satan perverts this by drawing man's soul to perform in systems he has created to emulate God. Unable to be in spiritual communion with the Lord, man is therefore encouraged to earn God's acceptance by living up to the dictates of these systems. You are no longer saved by being reconciled with God through the new birth available in Jesus Christ. Instead you are made righteous by belonging to a certain organization or by doing good works. The result is that man becomes religious instead of spiritual, and steeped in idolatry while being deceived into thinking he is serving the Lord. Organizations such as the Freemasons, Greek fraternities & sororities, etc. serve this same purpose: giving man something to worship, and a way to attain righteousness, apart from God.

We must realize that God is not looking for organizational faithfulness, but organic formation. Are you an organically grown son of God or have you just appended yourself to an organization which emulates the sons of God? In these last days, you must be sure. This is why God tells us to examine ourselves to see if we really are in the faith. The church you go to or the denomination to which you belong is really insignificant. You need to ask yourself, "Are you born again?" Is Christ being formed in your heart? Are you able to bear not only the fruit of Christ within you, but the gifts that come through the fruit? The power of God in your life confirms who and what you are, not verbal confession (1 Corinthians 2:4-5). This is the true presentation of the Gospel. It is the evidence of a manifested son in these last days.

Do not kid yourself, friend. Jesus has paved the way for us to not only know the truth, but to possess the truth so that we can be made free by it. Conversely, religion leaves you unsure and always wondering if you're saved, trying to pay your way into Heaven with good works. Life in the New Testament church is not about performance, but being transformed. Every Old Testament ordinance is fulfilled in Christ. There are no tithes, no Sabbath days, no holidays (holy days)...no outward performance at all. Christ in you is your hope of glory. Religion can only lead you to law as you perform on the outside instead of having Christ formed on the inside.

We all are faced with the same question: Am I performing for the religious traditions of men or am I being conformed to the image of Christ by the power of God? These two natures will struggle within us - the flesh versus the spirit; one is religious and the other has a relationship. Which one is happening in you?

The Law

> *Romans 6:11-14*
> *Likewise reckon ye also yourselves to be dead indeed unto sin, but alive unto God through Jesus Christ our Lord. Let not sin therefore reign in your mortal body, that ye should obey it in the lusts thereof. Neither yield ye your members as instruments of unrighteousness unto sin: but yield yourselves unto God, as those that are alive from the dead, and your members as instruments of righteousness unto God. For sin shall not have dominion over you: for ye are not under the law, but under grace. What then? Shall we sin, because we are not under the law, but under grace? God forbid. Know ye not, that to whom ye yield yourselves servants to obey, his servants ye are to whom ye obey; whether of sin unto death, or of obedience unto righteousness?*

One of the most detrimental things to your development as a Christian is to place yourself under the Old Testament law. Now I know many of you believe that the law is necessary in the Christian life, but the Bible says that we are not under law; we are under grace (Romans 6:14-15). God ordained grace as the means through which we receive new life and have His nature developed within us. This is why He says that sin will no longer have dominion over us because we are not under law, but under grace. You see, it did not require a nature change for man to receive God's law. In fact, the law was given by God precisely to restrain a nature man **could not** change. This is why no man could obey the law completely (Acts 15:10).

Even now there are those telling Christians that they must keep the law.

Yet, the Bible says that if you want to be under even one law, then you must do them all (James 2:10). The Ten Commandments are just the tip of the iceberg. In all, the law has 613 commands which Israel had to obey. You can keep the Sabbath day, but you are still behind by six hundred and twelve other laws which must be observed. Such persons had better be in their backyards every day offering up a bullock or a lamb. You had better have some turtle doves or pigeons to present when your daughter gets married. You can seek to observe every aspect of the law, yet you will never be made righteous by it (Hebrews 7:19). No one will ever make it into Heaven by observing the law for the Bible says that such is impossible.

You begin trying to keep the laws, but with the old nature still alive, you wind up in frustration and anxiety, unable to do the things God demands. Why? Because law cannot make you righteous (Romans 3:20-28; Galatians 2:16, 3:11). Rules and regulations cannot change what you are on the inside, and without such a change, all you are left with is religious performance. God is not looking for performance; He is looking for a people who are transformed to be like Him. Only then can we have an intimate relationship with Him inside of the Holy of Holies, not having to stand afar off in the outer court.

Now you can see why God gave Israel the law. The purpose of the law was not to perfect man, but to restrain sin in man while at the same time showing him the filthy reality of the flesh. The law was given to show us that our natural state is one of a sinner incapable of serving God. The law exposes me as a rebel because by nature I will rise up in disobedience once it is given. As the Scriptures say, the law stimulates sin in the fallen nature. When the law comes, sin revives, and we die (Romans 7:7-9).

The more you place yourself under law, the more you'll have a fight in you from the sin nature. Why? Because you are relying on your own effort to **perform** instead of God's ability to **transform**. We must realize that there is something in our flesh which wars against the things of God. This confirms that we are helpless against sin unless God's grace transforms us into another kind of creation. What God intends to be a schoolmaster to point us to our need for Jesus Christ will instead be used by the Devil to ensnare us and keep us trapped in sin if we do not understand this.

Colossians 2:8-19
Beware lest any man spoil you through philosophy and
vain deceit, after the tradition of men, after the rudiments
of the world, and not after Christ. For in him dwelleth all
the fulness of the Godhead bodily. And ye are complete
in him, which is the head of all principality and power: in

whom also ye are circumcised with the circumcision made without hands, in putting off the body of the sins of the flesh by the circumcision of Christ: buried with him in baptism, wherein also ye are risen with him through the faith of the operation of God, who hath raised him from the dead. And you, being dead in your sins and the uncircumcision of your flesh, hath he quickened together with him, having forgiven you all trespasses; blotting out the handwriting of ordinances that was against us, which was contrary to us, and took it out of the way, nailing it to his cross; and having spoiled principalities and powers, he made a shew of them openly, triumphing over them in it. Let no man therefore judge you in meat, or in drink, or in respect of an holyday, or of the new moon, or of the Sabbath days: which are a shadow of things to come; but the body is of Christ. Let no man beguile you of your reward in a voluntary humility and worshipping of angels, intruding into those things which he hath not seen, vainly puffed up by his fleshly mind, and not holding the Head, from which all the body by joints and bands having nourishment ministered, and knit together, increaseth with the increase of God.

Here in Colossians, the Apostle informs the church that no man has the right to judge us in terms of what we eat, what we drink, or what holiday (holy day) we observe. All of these Old Testament laws with their feast days and rituals are but a "*shadow*" of Christ (Colossians 2:14-17; Hebrews 10:1-10). They all point to Jesus Christ as the culmination of all the law because He is the substance and fulfillment of the law. When we are transformed into His image by being born again, we partake of Jesus' nature and are no longer lawbreakers. Because we now abide in Him, the life of Christ within us has become our righteousness.

All human effort is sin, whether attempting to do right or to do wrong, because it is born of the flesh and not the Spirit (Isaiah 64:6). God is not looking for us to try, but to bow our heads and die so that His Son may live through us. This is what it means to have entered the Sabbath rest, when we have ceased from our own efforts. There is freedom from works and from the law as we find rest for our souls by walking in the Spirit. The first requirement to obtaining this freedom is to recognize that we are helpless to overcome in our own effort. We need the Lord to build this house or else we labor in vain (Psalm 127:1).

The Old Testament is laws and external works; the New Testament is a person and inward transformation. Righteousness is now embodied in

47

Jesus Christ the Messiah, and you know what? The law was not made for a righteous man. Instead, the Bible says that the law was made for rebels, unholy people, adulterers, murderers, thieves, robbers, etc. (1 Timothy 1:9-10). **These** are the sort who need the law; those who are rebellious against God *by nature* because they have not been transformed.

Let's say for example that there is a state trooper parked on the interstate with a speed detection device. He is not there to catch those who are *not* speeding. He is there for the purpose of catching the lawbreakers. Further, if you are not speeding, the presence of the state trooper is of no significance to you. Hear me on this. There is no need for the law to monitor you with a radar gun because you are not seeking to break the law; the law is not there for **you**. It is the same when we are born again. There is no effort to try and obey rules because the Lord displaces that rebellious nature with His nature and the law of the Spirit. Since your new nature has no desire to rebel, there is never a need to apply the law.

Hebrews Chapter 9 says that the Old Testament laws cannot perfect you concerning your conscience. Your conscience is the part of you that God leaves intact for you to be saved. He'll prick your conscience to convict you and make you aware that you are doing wrong so that you will be ashamed of your sin. Without anyone telling you that you are doing wrong, your conscience will let you know. Jesus purges our conscience because He can do what the law could not: create a new nature within us that is not a rebel against Him. As a result, we can walk sincerely before the Lord in obedience to Him. No longer being in covenant with sin, we do not have to feel uncomfortable around Him because there is no hidden sin to which we are holding. Our consciences are clear. However, willful and continued disobedience can leave your conscience seared so that you no longer are receptive to the leadings of the Spirit to turn from sin (1 Timothy 4:1-2). You become hardened to the righteousness of God by your own continued rebellion.

Don't let anyone place you under the law. Doing so will rob you of your peace. It will also hinder your development of spiritual fruit, and make the war against the flesh that much more severe by stimulating it to rebel against God. The mechanics of the faith - bible study, prayer, fasting, obeying the word of God, etc. - are necessary to feed and mature the new nature within you. However, you are not doing these things to try to please God or earn His approval. You are just doing what is required to mortify that within you which is against God. God is not looking for you to have to do something for Him. He desires a nature that wants to serve Him willingly.

Law will not allow Jesus to be exalted because you are basing your salvation on what you do or don't do. True salvation is offering yourself sacrificially to God so that His nature grows out of you, bringing Jesus to the forefront. If we want Him to increase, then we must decrease (John 3:30). It is time to cast off the old in order to receive the new. We must eradicate Ishmael in order to receive Isaac. Exterminate Esau to receive Jacob. Kill Saul so that David can take the throne. Mortify the first Adam so that Jesus Christ, the last Adam, can be exalted and enthroned as the Lord of all flesh.

Kill the old man and you are free. That is good news! The old man was killed for us on Calvary. What must I do? Believe it! Identify yourself as being dead on the cross so that Christ may live. Only then can you walk in newness of life. God condemned sin in Jesus' flesh through His crucifixion. The sin nature from Adam was eradicated in Christ.

It's all about separation from the deeds and works of the law and believing in Christ. Why? He's purging the inside of you to house the Holy Spirit whom Adam lost. He's not interested in outward performance. Both the Jew and the Gentile are justified through faith. Through this inworking of belief, a transformation is taking place on the inside of us making us living expressions of faith. Such is how we establish the law because the law of the Spirit has changed the human heart from being that of a rebel into an obedient child of God. You do what is right by nature, not by compulsion, because you have been made into the image of God. We can then actually do the same works that the Messiah did with empowerment of the Holy Spirit.

Fear

> *2 Timothy 1:6-12*
> *Wherefore I put thee in remembrance that thou stir up the gift of God, which is in thee by the putting on of my hands. **For God hath not given us the spirit of fear; but of power, and of love, and of a sound mind**. Be not thou therefore ashamed of the testimony of our Lord, nor of me his prisoner: but be thou partaker of the afflictions of the gospel according to the power of God; who hath saved us, and called us with an holy calling, not according to our works, but according to his own purpose and grace, which was given us in Christ Jesus before the world began, but is now made manifest by the appearing of our Savior Jesus Christ, who hath abolished death and hath brought life and immortality to light through the gospel: whereunto I am appointed a preacher, and an apostle, and a teacher for the Gentiles. For the which cause I also suffer these things: nevertheless I am not ashamed: for I know whom*

I have believed, and am persuaded that he is able to keep
that which I have committed unto him against that day.

Everything from the world is designed to keep you away from God. If Satan cannot draw you to the world by lust, then he will use fear to keep you from the Spirit. Fear is one of the enemy's strongest weapons against a Christian's growth. The Devil paints himself as an indestructible behemoth who cannot fall or be destroyed. Like Goliath, he taunts the armies of God, daring the saints to come out and engage in conflict with him. Yet as with the armies of Israel, fear cripples the human mind and disempowers the soul for the battle.

Remember, fear does not come from God for He has not given us a spirit of fear, but of love, power, and a sound mind. Fear comes as we dwell upon the lying wonders in Satan's kingdom. It is the evidence that we have become self-conscious; focused on ourselves and our lives in this world. As a result, we fear what will happen to us if we really stand for Christ. We fear what we will be like if Christ forms in us. We fear what we will face by engaging in spiritual warfare with the Devil.

This is why most church folks are stymied and won't move one inch to confront anything. They are afraid of the Devil, and the Devil loves it to be so. Constantly, Satan is propagating images in the world to instill fear in man. You love scary movies, but you better know that scary movies love you too because through it, the devil is planting seeds of fear within to stop you. You watched scary movies and now you are unable to sleep at night. You are staring at your closet, straining to see if a face is looking back at you. Your knees are knocking together in your own bed imagining that you are hearing noises or seeing things. You pay the monthly note on your home, yet you are scared to death while in it. That is crazy! Look, why should you be the one scared? Just override what you feel and step up to the plate. Even if permitted by God, the Devil could only kill you once, so what is the big deal? Sudden death equals sudden glory. Satan is trying to scare the living daylights out of you based upon your own imaginations. Remember, the first to go to hell in Revelation are the fearful and unbelieving (Revelation 21:8).

The spirit of bondage will not let you be led by the Spirit of God because you are still bound to the flesh (Romans 8:12-15). The flesh is afraid of spiritual things. Just consider how abnormal that is. You are a spirit, but you are afraid of spirits. So what does the Devil do? He threatens you with spiritual things. That is why you see things in your room at night, paralyzed in the bed while feeling like something is holding you down. The Devil is trying to terrify you so that you won't want to go into the spirit realm. I woke up one night to find the television playing, but the television was turned off. I was seeing images on the television screen. I said, *"Devil stop fooling around with the TV. I am trying to get some sleep."* Don't get all shook up about it; it is only the devil. What is the big deal? Why should you be afraid of him when you are the son of God?

Fear is sin because God has not given us a spirit of fear. If we hold on to fear, it is because we do not have faith in God and His Word. When we succumb to fear, we are essentially believing in the Devil and his power more than God. We can't feed on fear and have faith in God at the same time. According to Scripture, this is all due to one root cause.

> *Hebrews 2:14-15*
> *Forasmuch then as the children are partakers of flesh and blood, he also himself likewise took part of the same; that through death he might destroy him that had the power of death, that is, the devil; and deliver them who through **fear of death** were all their lifetime subject to bondage.*

In order for Christians to walk in the power of God, they must overcome the fear of death. The fear of dying is what makes you subject to enslavement by the Devil. There is not only fear of dying physically, but there is fear about dying to this world. Why? Because you still care about your reputation in this world and what people think of you.

In dying to the flesh, we are crucified to this world, even while living as strangers and pilgrims in the earth. Fear stops the organic growth of Christ's nature in you as a protective mechanism of the flesh. Your flesh does not want to be crucified. It instinctively knows that if Christ were to manifest in you, the world will hate you just as it hated Him. We see in Matthew Chapter 13 that the sower sows the word, and as the word begins to grow, tribulation comes. Man then begins to back away from the word in order to prevent it from bearing fruit. Most people don't want to be hated, ostracized, or not liked by their peers.

Having been created to be in the image of God, man is innately aware that something is missing inside of him. Outside of Christ, we live our entire existence trying to fill this void; seeking to be accepted, to fit in, or to belong to something. This search for an identity is what makes you susceptible to the domination and control of man because the root cause for all fear is rejection. That is why the Bible says the fear of man bringeth about a snare to the soul (Proverbs 29:25).

However, when we are born again, our identity is now found in Christ (Acts 17:28). We are no longer a part of this culture for we are not of this world. As a result, we do not live by our own desires; we do not do what we want to do or go where we want to go. We don't say what we want to say, dress how we want to dress, or hang around with whom we choose. If we have been born again of incorruptible seed by the will God and of the Holy Spirit, then it is the will of God which compels us and not our own.

> *2 Corinthians 5:14-15*
> *For **the love of Christ constraineth us**; because we thus judge, that if one died for all, then were all dead: And that he died for all, **that they which live should not henceforth live unto themselves, but unto him** which died for them, and rose again.*

Fear is designed to hinder you from bringing forth Christ within you. The only answer to conquering fear is to finally face it and die! Get up on the cross with Christ and be crucified with Him. Logically, you cannot kill a dead man. Once you mortify your flesh, the fear of death will be eliminated from your life. What I'm saying cannot be theoretical or just another religious catchphrase. This actually has to happen to you. You must be crucified with Christ to get victory over the spirit of fear. Otherwise, your life will be filled with torment because with fear comes torment (1 John 4:18).

Whatever you do my friend, don't fall prey to fear. Get on the cross and stay there until the nature of fear is mortified, and you come out free in resurrection life and resurrection power.

The Seventeen Works of the Flesh

> *Galatians 5:16-21:*
> *This I say then, Walk in the Spirit, and ye shall not fulfill the lust of the flesh. For the flesh lusteth against the Spirit, and the Spirit against the flesh: and these are contrary the one to the other: so that ye cannot do the things that ye would. But if ye be led of the Spirit, ye are not under the law. Now the works of the flesh are manifest, which are these: **adultery, fornication, uncleanness, lasciviousness, idolatry, witchcraft, hatred, variance, emulations, wrath, strife, seditions, heresies, envyings, murders, drunkenness, revellings, and such like**: of the which I tell you before, as I have also told you in time past, that they which do such things shall not inherit the kingdom of God.*

Seed Sown Amongst the Thorns

Since the fall, Satan has planted and cultivated in man the seed of rebellion. This fallen, Adamic nature is reflected in seventeen works of the flesh, representing attributes that make a human anti-God and anti-Christ. We must destroy these works in order to bring forth nine fruits of the Spirit. This can only be done as we crucify the fallen nature within us. As the text says, those who belong to Christ **have crucified** the flesh along with its affections and lusts. The old nature must be mortified to allow the new nature to take hold.

This is the conflict in which every member of the Body of Christ is engaged. Who is going to confront that which is within them? Who is willing to do what is necessary to destroy those strongholds in us which make us uninhabitable by God? You confront the old man through fasting, prayer, bible study, and disciplined obedience to God until it is dead. With these seventeen works of the flesh alive, the nature of Christ cannot come to fruition in us. The seventeen works of the flesh are the weeds, tares, and kudzu which seek to strangle off your life in Christ. This is why the flesh must be mortified. Remember, if you don't crucify the flesh, then the flesh will crucify Christ in you.

There is no mystery involved here. It's a simple process. Sanctify yourself from the world, commit yourself to God, and do the mechanics necessary to destroy that which was once compelling you to sin against God. Christ in us is our only hope of escaping the wrath to come in the not so distant future, and making it to a home called Heaven.

We all know that something had control over us before we were saved. A lot of us have pretended for years, but it is time for someone to go through the process of sanctification unto holiness. Only then will we see the Lord move in a supernatural way in these last days. If you want to be free, do not look for the problems to be outside of you. Jesus plainly said that there is nothing on the outside of a man that could defile him, but the things that can defile a man are on the inside (Mark 7:15). We have to deal with what is on the inside. An internal war is necessary if we ever want to live in eternal bliss with the Lord. It's time to deal with the inner court and cleanse ourselves from double-mindedness to see God move like never before. I am glad we've come to the kingdom for such a time as this.

Ahab and Jezebel

Revelation 2:12-26
And to the angel of the church in Pergamos write; These things saith he which hath the sharp sword with two edges; I know thy works, and where thou dwellest, even where

53

Satan's seat is: and thou holdest fast my name, and hast not denied my faith, even in those days wherein Antipas was my faithful martyr, who was slain among you, where Satan dwelleth. But I have a few things against thee, because thou hast there them that hold the doctrine of **Balaam, who taught Balac to cast a stumblingblock before the children of Israel, to eat things sacrificed unto idols, and to commit fornication.**

So hast thou also them that hold the doctrine of the Nicolaitans, which thing I hate. Repent; or else I will come unto thee quickly, and will fight against them with the sword of my mouth. He that hath an ear, let him hear what the Spirit saith unto the churches; To him that overcometh will I give to eat of the hidden manna, and will give him a white stone, and in the stone a new name written, which no man knoweth saving he that receiveth it.

And unto the angel of the church in Thyatira write; these things saith the Son of God, who hath his eyes like unto a flame of fire, and his feet are like fine brass; I know thy works, and charity, and service, and faith, and thy patience, and thy works; and the last to be more than the first. Notwithstanding I have a few things against thee, because thou sufferest **that woman Jezebel,** *which calleth herself a prophetess,* **to teach and to seduce my servants to commit fornication, and to eat things sacrificed unto idols.** *And I gave her space to repent of her fornication; and she repented not.*

Behold, I will cast her into a bed, and them that commit adultery with her into great tribulation, except they repent of their deeds. And I will kill her children with death; and all the churches shall know that I am he which searcheth the reins and hearts: and I will give unto every one of you according to your works. But unto you I say, and unto the rest in Thyatira, as many as have not this doctrine, and which have not known the depths of Satan, as they speak; I will put upon you none other burden. But that which ye have already hold fast till I come. And he that overcometh, and keepeth my works unto the end, to him will I give power over the nations.

In Revelation Chapter 2, God cites two individuals with contaminating the Church: Balaam and Jezebel. While both persons are literal figures historically, in this text God is dealing with the spirit operating within them. Notice that **both** are blamed for leading God's servants to commit fornication and eat things sacrificed to idols. Balaam was a prophet who taught Israel's enemies to ensnare them in idolatry via illicit sexual practices so that he could receive the wages of unrighteousness (Numbers Chapters 22-25; 2 Peter 2:15; Jude 1:11). Jezebel was a witch and a whore who used false authority to lead Israel into the worship of Baal (I Kings 16:31, 18:4, 19:1-2).

One *abdicates authority* and manipulates others so as to enjoy worldly comforts, while the other *usurps authority* and uses witchcraft/seduction to receive worship. They are two sides of the same coin. In each case, it was submission to whoredoms - both physically and spiritually - which joined God's people to Baal and brought about their downfall.

Such is the nature of fallen man, as seen in what Adam and Eve became through sin. In eating the forbidden fruit in the Garden of Eden, Adam and Eve experienced a role reversal. Adam, who was created to be the head, became submissive to his wife. Eve, who was created to submit to Adam, instead became the authority for him in place of God. It was giving his God-given authority over to Eve which God saw as Adam's greatest transgression (Genesis 3:17). The protection and covering God had established for mankind in patriarchy was supplanted with matriarchy, leaving mankind vulnerable to Satan and alienated from the life of the Spirit.

We have seen these spirits continue to manifest down through time as men forsake the place God has given to them in deference to matriarchal authority. Samson and Delilah, David and Bathsheba, and of course, Ahab and Jezebel are reflections of this perversion. As seen in God's words to the Churches at Pergamos and Thyatira, these perverse spirits are still alive and well today.

Jezebel literally means "unchaste" and "married to Baal". This spirit is one of the most diabolical birthed out of the kingdom of Hell. According to Scripture, Jezebel became the wife of Ahab, king of Israel, and set up idolatrous groves undergirded by her own priests to lead the people into worshipping Baal. She was able to exert this illegitimate rule and influence over the kingdom of Israel because Ahab in essence abdicated his authority to her. To release the Israelites from her captivity, God had to finally destroy Jezebel, who the Bible says was a witch and a whore (2 Kings 9:22). Similarly, if left unconfronted, this spirit will sit in the church propagating its unlawful and unordained rulership. The spirit of Jezebel wars against your freedom as it attempts to control, manipulate, and dominate you. Remember, I am not talking about physical women or men (Ephesians 6:12). We are dealing with **spirits**. The Jezebel and Ahab spirits show forth via masculine women and effeminate men. These witchcraft working spirits are sorcerers and controllers, seeking to stop your progression in God.

Friends, a lot of what I'm about to say may be controversial. Nevertheless it is true, so we must accept it. The Bible is clear that leadership in the church is ordained and given into the hands of men who have been qualified by God to lead. Church authority is to be a reflection of who God is: a Father. Patriarchy was established by God specifically to organically grow out of us the nature necessary to fellowship with Him. He is the logos and does everything with precision and reasoning. Being brought up under the tutelage of one who **demonstrates fatherhood** serves as a pattern for God's children in how to relate to Him as our Father. God used this same principle when sending His Son.

Jesus came to reveal God to us as Father, serving as a forerunner for us (John 8:19; John 14:7-10). Jesus only did what He saw His Father doing, submitting His will to the Father's in all things. When Jesus chose individuals to serve as the foundational leadership of His Church, He again followed His Father's example and chose men who could reflect a father's authority. Jesus understood that knowing God as a Father was essential to us being reconciled to Him. This is why the last text of the Old Testament says of the spirit of Elijah:

> *Malachi 4:6*
> *And he shall turn the heart of the fathers to the children,*
> *and the heart of the children to their fathers, lest I come*
> *and smite the earth with a curse.*

Most of the curses which have come upon mankind result from the fact that we have been raised under matriarchy (Isaiah 3:1-26). Instead of coming to know God through the heart of a father, matriarchy inwardly conforms us to seek a feminine presentation of God. Since this is the only type of authority we know, we will by nature repel from the character of God the Father, choosing the comfort and seeming normality of submitting to an Ahab/ Jezebel spirit. It produces a perverted view of God where you are unable to identify or walk with Jesus Christ. Whether you have someone shirking responsibility or another usurping it, the result is that the image of true authority is perverted. They are two sides of the same coin and both result in God's people being led into fornication and idolatry.

Although the very nature of God is that of a Patriarch, the Jezebel spirit stands up and says, "*No! I will not accept or receive God as a Father. I will remake God into the image of a woman - or at the very least an effeminate man - so that I can receive worship for myself and have the people serve me."* What is an effeminate man? It is a man who chooses the pleasures, comforts, and pampering of the flesh over the arduous role of servanthood through leadership and engaging in war with the enemy. Such men have no backbone or intestinal fortitude to stand against what's wrong and represent that which is right. To protect the people against this perverted representation of who and what God is, the Apostles were careful to give precise instructions regarding the qualifications for Church leadership.

> *Titus 1:5-10:*
> *For this cause left I thee in Crete, that thou shouldest set in order the things that are wanting, and ordain elders in every city, as I had appointed thee: if any be blameless, **the husband of one wife**, having faithful children not accused of riot or unruly. For a bishop must be blameless, as the steward of God; not self-willed, not soon angry, not given to wine, no striker, not given to filthy lucre; but a lover of hospitality, a lover of good men, sober, just, holy, temperate; holding fast the faithful word as he hath been taught, that he may be able by sound doctrine both to exhort and to convince the gainsayers. For there are many unruly and vain talkers and deceivers, specially they of the circumcision.*

> *1 Timothy 3:1-13:*
> *This is a true saying, If a man desire the office of a bishop, he desireth a good work. A bishop then must be blameless, **the husband of one wife**, vigilant, sober, of good behaviour, given to hospitality, apt to teach; not given to wine, no striker, not greedy of filthy lucre; but patient, not a brawler, not covetous; one that ruleth well his own house, having his children in subjection with all gravity; (**for if a man know not how to rule his own house, how shall he take care of the church of God?**) not a novice, lest being lifted up with pride he fall into the condemnation of the devil. Moreover he must have a good report of them which are without; lest he fall into reproach and the snare of the devil. Likewise must the deacons be grave, not double-tongued, not given to much wine, not greedy of filthy lucre; holding the mystery of the faith in a pure conscience. And let these also first be proved; then let them use the office of a deacon, being*

found blameless. Even so must their wives be grave, not slanderers, sober, faithful in all things. Let the deacons be the husbands of one wife, ruling their children and their own houses well. For they that have used the office of a deacon well purchase to themselves a good degree, and great boldness in the faith which is in Christ Jesus.

In both of these Scriptures, the Apostle Paul outlines the qualifications for elders, overseers, and deacons, including that they **must** be the husband of one wife. Who can debate this? God's qualifications stand sure. Those ordained as leaders in the Church must be the husband of one wife because one must prove himself able to lead his *own* family before he can take care of *God's* family, which is the Church. The root of the word "family" is the same as the root for "father", which is the Greek word *pater*. Without a "pater" there is no family. The only one whose genetic makeup and birthright qualifies for being a father is a man, as testified by Scripture.

God has always chosen patriarchs to reflect His heart to His people (1 Samuel 13:14; Jeremiah 3:15; Acts 13:22). In setting up men after his own heart, God ensures that this same patriarchal heart is imparted to those being fed by them. Whether male or female, the more we come to know the Lord, the more our hearts are prepared to receive and appreciate the authority of God as our Father. Conversely, the more we sit under matriarchy, the more our hearts are conformed to that which is against God, until even the very character of God seems foreign to us.

If we are to move into perfection and see the manifestation of the nature of Christ out of us, we must confront these spirits and tear down the altars they have built within us. In these last days, God is looking for people who will make a stand against Baal. As the prophet Elijah of old, the proclamation is being made: if God be God, then serve Him; but if Baal is god, then serve him (1 Kings 18:21). Let's find out just who this God is and make up our minds once and for all.

This system of false authority is being projected like no other time in history. Through radical feminism, the media, and a Babylonian religious system, the world is projecting its hatred of the Father. Only those who have the will and determination to stand for God in austere times will be able to conquer this spirit. It is a renegade out of control, and the only way to overcome it is through death. My counsel to you is not to try to stand against these spirits of Jezebel and Ahab, but offer yourself up to God as a living sacrifice, holy and acceptable unto Him. Let the fires of Pentecost burn in your soul as God shows Himself strong for you and in you by His Spirit coming upon you.

Seed Sown Amongst the Thorns

We must realize that these times are desperate. Believe me, the old cliché stands sure: desperate times call for desperate measures. The fires of Pentecost must burn again in the Christian church and in the Christians' hearts. We have no other answer, no other choice. The weapons formed against us are too powerful. Only God can win this war as He is organically grown out of His Body, filling us with His nature and character. Only when He has vessels fit for His use will He go to war through you and me to destroy the intruders who have come into the gates of His Church (2 Timothy 2:21). Will you volunteer for the Master's use?

This page intentionally left blank.

Chapter 4 - Incorruptible Seed

Seed Coming to Fruition

> *Matthew 13:1-9:*
> *The same day went Jesus out of the house, and sat by the sea side. And great multitudes were gathered together unto him, so that he went into a ship, and sat; and the whole multitude stood on the shore. And he spake many things unto them in parables, saying, Behold, a sower went forth to sow; and when he sowed, some seeds fell by the way side, and the fowls came and devoured them up: some fell upon stony places, where they had not much earth: and forthwith they sprung up, because they had no deepness of earth: and when the sun was up, they were scorched; and because they had no root, they withered away. And some fell among thorns; and the thorns sprung up, and choked them: but other fell into good ground, and brought forth fruit, some an hundredfold, some sixtyfold, some thirtyfold. Who hath ears to hear, let him hear.*

In the above text, Jesus explains the parable of the sower. This parable is a basic illustration of how the Gospel of Jesus Christ is an **organic** gospel. To understand the Gospel, one must first know that its fundamental elements are rooted and grounded in agriculture. The Bible itself is an agricultural book written from the book of Genesis (the conception of life) to Revelation (the manifestation of that which was conceived). Similarly, the Gospel is designed to plant the nature of Christ in believers and then grow that nature out of them over time so that the life of Christ is manifest from within to the world. This is the missing link in most ministries today. You have preachers who do not understand the Gospel trying to teach others who don't possess the life of Christ within how to live it out. The only thing which can result from this is the continued failure and frustration of religious performance.

The Bible outlines the budding to life of a seed - a nature - which God originally planted in Adam. The purpose of this seed was to fill the earth with a creation made in God's own image (Genesis 1:26-28). God breathed into Adam the breath of life and he became a living soul. However, Adam fell into rebellion and died to God's presence as the Holy Spirit departed from him. Yet, this was not the end of that seed. The Bible says that unless a seed dies, it cannot bring forth life. Although man became dead to God as his nature was corrupted by sin, Jesus appeared centuries later to reignite that life by bringing back to man the Holy Spirit which Adam lost. In making a way for man to be born again by the Spirit and become partakers of the divine nature, Jesus restored to man what He took not away (Psalm 69:4; 2 Peter 1:4). This was the prophecy written about Jesus through the lips of David, the psalmist. It is the impartation of the divine nature which allows the Christian to be metamorphosized into the very image of the Christ. Without that nature, there is no salvation. No matter what you do as a professing Christian, you have no right to enter into fellowship with the living God unless you have been born again to possess His nature.

God is seeking to organically grow His nature out of the human heart so that He may have communion with us again. This is why salvation is not based upon what we can or cannot do; it is not dependent upon our abilities. It is the grace of God through Jesus Christ, imparting a nature to us and thereby changing us into the image of God in Christ. Only then can God receive us and re-establish a covenant of love with us, His adopted sons and daughters.

The Seed is the Word of God

> *John 6:63*
> *It is the spirit that quickeneth; the flesh profiteth nothing: the words that I speak unto you, they are spirit, and they are life.*

The fact that the Gospel is to be organically grown out of man is completely indiscernible and incomprehensible to the carnal mind. Yet, there it is in Scripture as plain as day in Matthew Chapter 13. The sower going out to sow seed is a picture of God sowing His word into the hearts of humanity. Some "seed" fell by the way side (meaning they never enter into salvation), some on stony places, some on thorns, and some on good ground.

Friends, you must understand that the word of God brings the life of God to bear on the human heart. In order for this seed to take root, the word must fall on good ground. The mind must be pliable and receptive, and the heart must be open to change. Like a baby conceived in a mother's womb, the word that was planted must then gestate through growth cycles into maturity to bring forth the nature of Christ into manifestation. It is then that you will become a manifested son of God and not just a confessing or professing Christian in name only (John 17:6; Romans 8:19; 1 John 1:2).

Under the guise of being Godly ministers, many are deceiving people into thinking they can come to God in their own self-righteousness. This is a damnable heresy at its very essence. You cannot keep the fallen Adamic nature, add Jesus to it, and be saved. Such is a lie born in Hell, conceived by the Devil to destroy millions on a global scale. Jesus says that the word can fall by the way side and even be plucked out of the heart once it has been sown. Take a look at His explanation of the parable.

Matthew 13:18-23
Hear ye therefore the parable of the sower. When any one heareth the word of the kingdom, and understandeth it not, then cometh the wicked one, and catcheth away that which was sown in his heart. This is he which received seed by the way side. But he that received the seed into stony places, the same is he that heareth the word, and anon with joy receiveth it; yet hath he not root in himself, but dureth for a while: for when tribulation or persecution ariseth because of the word, by and by he is offended. He also that received seed among the thorns is he that heareth the word; and the care of this world, and the deceitfulness of riches, choke the word, and he becometh unfruitful. But he that received seed into the good ground is he that heareth the word, and understandeth it; which also beareth fruit, and bringeth forth, some an hundredfold, some sixty, some thirty.

The first hearers are described as those who receive the word without understanding, allowing the seed to fall by the way side as the adversary comes to catch it away. The next hearer is initially joyful about the word, but receives it in a stony place. With uncircumsized and stony hearts, these will not yield to the word sown because they have not been born again. As a result, the word cannot take root; the root is discipline. The Bible says they endure for a while, but they have no stick-to-it-iveness; no commitment, dedication, or fervent desire to see that word come forth with power. When persecution arises because of the word that has been placed within them, they are offended and fall away. Note that Jesus makes no mention of God going to bring that person back. We must have good soil - a repentant heart - in order to become disciples, staying under God's leadership and correction, in order to enter in (Luke 14:27; Hebrews 5:9).

The next person who receives the word does so among the thorns. He hears the word and new life starts to grow in him, but the deceitfulness of riches choke it off so that he becomes unfruitful. Let me take the time to say this to you. Those of you who have been deceived by prosperity doctrines, take heed. That doctrine of devils is choking off the very word God has sent to save your soul. It is preached in order to focus your mind on things in the earth and not on God (Colossians 3:2). The hypocrites and liars preaching this perversion try to cover their tracks by telling you the finances are used to bring the Gospel around the world. Well first of all, they would have to be preaching the real Gospel of the Kingdom for that to be true. Instead, what they are actually preaching is greed, avarice, covetousness, and a selfish "get all you can for yourself" mentality (1 Timothy 6:3-5). If this were not true friends, then why would they need a Rolls-Royce, Lear jet, and a two-million-dollar home? How are these things necessary in order to spread the Gospel around the world? Many people need to simply wake up out of this comatose condition and realize that they have been bewitched. The only option is to repent and turn to the true and living God so that this "prosperity" filth can be cleaned out of your souls.

Do not let the sown word of God be choked off in your life because you still love this present evil world and the prince who rules it, Satan. In the New Testament, there are two Greek words for the word "world": *aion* and *kosmos*. The word *aion* refers to the time and space arena in which we live; the ages, years, months, weeks, days, hours, and minutes which make up daily activities on this planet. The word *kosmos* addresses the fashions and allures of the world. We get words like cosmopolitan and cosmetics from it. It represents all of the things people glory in about the world - entertainment, music, dancing, drinking, drugs, etc. It includes all of the debauchery, fun, and glitz that is leading millions to Hell. A love for this world and all of its trappings choke off the word so that it becomes unfruitful. This is why it is so dangerous. God's design is for us to receive the word and bear fruit.

You Shall Know Them by Their Fruit

> *Galatians 5:22-26*
> *But the fruit of the Spirit is love, joy, peace, longsuffering, gentleness, goodness, faith, meekness, temperance: against such there is no law. And they that are Christ's have crucified the flesh with the affections and lusts. If we live in the Spirit, let us also walk in the Spirit. Let us not be desirous of vain glory, provoking one another, envying one another.*

There are nine fruits of the Spirit: love, joy, peace, longsuffering, gentleness, goodness, faith, meekness, and temperance. Against these nine fruits, there is no law. Examine what it says in verse 24, *"They that are Christ's have crucified the flesh with the affections and lusts."* Paul is telling the Galatians that those who really belong to Christ and are truly His Bride have killed the old carnal nature along with its desires and lusts. When the text says that we must crucify the "affections" of the flesh, it is the Greek word *pathema* and references that which stimulates the flesh to produce an emotional response.

Most preachers don't want you to crucify the flesh because they use the lusts of your flesh to keep you controllable. As a result, they preach sermons which cater to the flesh. They have mastered emotional manipulation so as to make their congregations feel loved, even while keeping them soulish and unable to manifest the life of Christ. It is the greatest delusion on the face of the earth because if you're going to be fruitful in reproducing after your own kind to bring forth Christians into the kingdom of God, you must first understand that love is not primarily an emotion or a feeling. We need to view love from God's perspective and not man's.

> *1 John 4:7-8*
> *Beloved, let us love one another: for love is of God; and every one that loveth is born of God, and knoweth God. He that loveth not knoweth not God; for God is love.*

The Bible does not say that God feels love. It plainly says that God is love. For me to have love I must possess the One who is love, and the only one in the universe who is love is God. When I attempt to feel or receive some emotional form of love from a human perspective, it becomes defiled. If I want to love, I must be filled with God because God is love. Humans love conditionally. God's love exists unconditionally because that is what He is. It is not what He does or feels, it is who He is. It is the essence of His very nature.

You cannot go out into this war with Satan being led by your emotions because Satan will use them to destroy you. You can work your fingers to the bone, but you will basically just drive yourself up a wall trying to "show love" to somebody who is full of the devil and does not want it. They will use your misguided zeal to take from you. Like leeches and parasites, they will drain all of your resources (time, money, effort, etc.), but they will be unable to truly receive love until God draws them.

This is why so many people on a worldwide scale labor trying to do good deeds. People will work in an elderly home, feed the hungry, serve in monasteries, become priests or nuns, etc. Some will perform acts of penance such as becoming like Mother Theresa, washing the sores of lepers in India. They whip themselves at Easter time to prove that they are submitting to the cross. They will do anything to punish themselves for the wicked things they've done, putting on outward displays of holiness so as to appear righteous to men. Muslims wrap themselves in all kinds of gowns and veils. There are those who will shave their heads bald or are living in destitution trying to prove that they're meek, humble, mild, and gentle. All of these things go on daily as men try to show love, not knowing that such is impossible.

You cannot show love, but you must **become** love. It is organically grown out of you as the nature of Jesus Christ is birthed within you. Read it for yourself in Galatians Chapter 5; one of the fruits of the Spirit is love. All you have to do is what a gardener does: tend to the seed the Lord has sown and bring it to maturity. When the crop is mature, you will be love. You won't have to feel love or act like you care; you will be love. The love in you will care for others all by itself.

We have too much human intervention in the processes that God has ordained to generate new life in us. Too many people are trying to make you conform to their definition of what you should be instead of feeding you God's word so that Christ can be formed in you. When Jesus was dealing with Peter about being a minister, He did not give him a bunch of laws, history, and denominational guidance. He asked him three times "Peter, do you love me?" Peter said, "Yes, I love you." Jesus said, "Feed my lambs. Feed my sheep. Feed my sheep." (John 21:15-17).

The Gospel has been perverted on a global scale. The only hope for man is that God raises up a remnant which He has birthed to reflect the nature of His Son; sons and daughters brought to maturity whom He can use to reach a lost and dying world.

Organic Growth vs. Organized Flesh

The sower sows the word. The Bible says everything about this sown word is agricultural. It is not based on laws, rules, rituals, and trying to conform to someone's presentation of God. God is growing a garden.

> *1 Corinthians 3:1-17*
> *And I, brethren, could not speak unto you as unto spiritual,*
> *but as unto carnal, even as unto babes in Christ. I have fed*
> *you with milk, and not with meat: for hitherto ye were not*
> *able to bear it, neither yet now are ye able. For ye are yet*
> *carnal: for whereas there is among you envying, and strife,*

and divisions, are ye not carnal, and walk as men? For while one saith, I am of Paul; and another, I am of Apollos; are ye not carnal? Who then is Paul, and who is Apollos, but ministers by whom ye believed, even as the Lord gave to every man? I have planted, Apollos watered; but God gave the increase. So then neither is he that planteth any thing, neither he that watereth; but God that giveth the increase. Now he that planteth and he that watereth are one: and every man shall receive his own reward according to his own labour. For we are labourers together with God: ye are God's husbandry [meaning garden], ye are God's building. According to the grace of God which is given unto me, as a wise masterbuilder, I have laid the foundation, and another buildeth thereon. But let every man take heed how he buildeth thereupon. For other foundation can no man lay than that is laid, which is Jesus Christ. Now if any man build upon this foundation gold, silver, precious stones, wood, hay, stubble; every man's work shall be made manifest: for the day shall declare it, because it shall be revealed by fire; and the fire shall try every man's work of what sort it is. If any man's work abide which he hath built thereupon, he shall receive a reward. If any man's work shall be burned, he shall suffer loss: but he himself shall be saved; yet so as by fire. Know ye not that ye are the temple of God, and that the Spirit of God dwelleth in you? If any man defile the temple of God, him shall God destroy; for the temple of God is holy, which temple ye are.

Paul is speaking in organic terms as he admonishes the Corinthian Church for getting caught up in the personalities of men. He says the people are carnal because they are filled with envy, strife, and divisions. What causes all of these divisions and strife? Schisms. They have denominationalized themselves. Some were followers of Paul, others of Apollos, some of Peter; everybody had to have their own little clique.

This is exactly what has happened in this present generation, folks. It is the desire for conformity to, and acceptance from, this present day religious structure which disempowers the masses. Denominations have scattered the flock, and every tribe has its own little gimmick. Seventh Day Adventists believe Saturday is the Sabbath day. Another group believes you can only baptize in the name of Jesus, while others say you must baptize in the name of the Father, Son, and Holy Ghost. Some say all signs, wonders, miracles, and gifts of the Holy Ghost have ceased, but others believe these things are still for today.

These divisions happen when man's carnal mind tries to have a private interpretation of the word of God instead of receiving the revelation of it from the Holy Spirit (2 Peter 1:20-21). The revelation of the Holy Spirit can only come through a relationship with God and you must possess the nature of God to have a relationship with Him (Romans 8:14). The more of Him which has been grown in you, the closer the relationship you will have with Him and the more you will know Him. This is why the Gospel is organic. God's seed must be sown in you, germinated, and brought into maturity for manifestation. Only then can God deal with the real you instead of this make believe you which the Devil makes you become in religion.

You see friends, a lot of preachers are building on a perverted foundation. The foundation of the Gospel is Jesus Christ, and Him crucified. That is it. Unless you come to Christ crucified, you have the wrong Gospel. God's way of delivering us is mortifying one nature through the crucifixion of Christ and resurrecting another nature as Jesus comes out of the tomb to impart eternal life to us. Not knowing this will keep us carnal, fleshly, sensual, and under the yoke of the Devil. We will be caught up in a Satanic delusion of just doing Christian works. You and I must die in Christ to be accounted worthy to escape the destruction coming on this planet.

It's time to open your eyes and realize that the Gospel is organic from beginning to end. The sower sows the word down into you to bring forth in due season a fruitful harvest: love, joy, peace, longsuffering, goodness, gentleness, meekness, temperance, and faith. The very nature of Christ is developed in you through the washing of the water by the word of God which cleanses you from all the filth of sin (Ephesians 5:26). This renovates the inner man and transforms your mind as you are made into a new creature who is prepared to be joined with your Bridegroom, Jesus Christ. You will then be made free from this decaying, God-forsaken world.

Remember, Jesus says it is a straight and narrow way that leads to Heaven, and a broad way that leads to damnation where many will go in thereat (Matthew 7:13-14). This should let you know that the likelihood of being saved is very slim in comparison to being damned. How far away are we from this reality? How far away have we wandered from the truth? Either you are bound to an institution of organized flesh as you try to live up to the dictates of men or you have you been organically conceived by God as His son and are manifesting the fruit of His nature within you. All of the earth is in birth pains, awaiting that manifestation even now (Romans 8:19). Only organic growth leads to sonship.

A Godly Seed

The mystery of God is found in three stages: conception, gestation, and manifestation. Those who are religious will have a hard time understanding what I am saying. However, if you mean business with the Lord and study His word, then this is the finest hour of your life as God begins the process of casting out the tares and gathering in the wheat.

There is something within us which has to be **put to death** in order for God to take hold of us. Once the seed is sown on good ground, the new nature we receive buds to life producing fruit as that old nature is crucified. One nature can only grow at the expense of the other. As He purifies your soul, God will eliminate the last few bondages and idiosyncrasies within you which are against Him; the things which make you unacceptable to Him. He will purify the double-mind, freeing you from what has been binding you all these years. The soulish cholesterol which has been holding you back will be removed so that the spirit man can come up to full stature. It is time for that which has been sown to come forth in power! Then our fruit will produce a spiritual harvest; some thirty, some sixty, and some one hundred fold (Matthew 13:8). Why not go for the gusto and produce a one hundred fold crop for God, destroying the Devil's kingdom and his works (1 John 3:2-8)?

We are now the sons of God, even though it does not yet appear what we shall be. There's another nature taking hold of you, changing your thoughts, perceptions and desires as you are conformed to Christ. If you are a Christian, this world should be growing strangely dim to you. Can't you see there is no hope here? There is no hope in politics, financial systems, or religion. Everything is decaying, including man. In the midst of this, God is seeking to reproduce a Godly seed after His own kind. Yet, is God reproducing in you? In order for that to occur, we must be partakers of His life.

> *John 15:1-17*
> *I am the true vine, and my Father is the husbandman. Every branch in me that beareth not fruit he taketh away: and every branch that beareth fruit, he purgeth it, that it may bring forth more fruit. Now ye are clean through the word which I have spoken unto you. Abide in me, and I in you. As the branch cannot bear fruit of itself, except it abide in the vine; no more can ye, except ye abide in me. I am the vine, ye are the branches: He that abideth in me, and I in him, the same bringeth forth much fruit: for without me ye can do nothing. If a man abide not in me, he is cast forth as*

a branch, and is withered; and men gather them, and cast them into the fire, and they are burned. If ye abide in me, and my words abide in you, ye shall ask what ye will, and it shall be done unto you. Herein is my Father glorified, that ye bear much fruit; so shall ye be my disciples. As the Father hath loved me, so have I loved you: continue ye in my love. If ye keep my commandments, ye shall abide in my love; even as I have kept my Father's commandments, and abide in his love. These things have I spoken unto you, that my joy might remain in you, and that your joy might be full. This is my commandment, That ye love one another, as I have loved you. Greater love hath no man than this, that a man lay down his life for his friends. Ye are my friends, if ye do whatsoever I command you. Henceforth I call you not servants; for the servant knoweth not what his lord doeth: but I have called you friends; for all things that I have heard of my Father I have made known unto you. Ye have not chosen me, but I have chosen you, and ordained you, that ye should go and bring forth fruit, and that your fruit should remain: that whatsoever ye shall ask of the Father in my name, he may give it you. These things I command you, that ye love one another.

Jesus speaks organically in this text, comparing Himself to a vine and us as the branches. As with any plant, all of the nutrients needed to sustain its life are found in the soil. Through the root, the vine is able to provide life to all of its branches. This is why it is so critical that we abide in Christ. Jesus says that we must abide (live) in Him and He must abide (live) in us. This is the only way that we can continue to have the life of God flowing through us.

Look at this closely. We bear good fruit, not through human effort, but by abiding in Jesus Christ. That way, the life of the Holy Spirit which Jesus possesses is imparted to us organically as the fruit of the Spirit develop naturally. There is nothing we can do to produce fruit on our own apart from abiding in Him. Find yourself impatient? Abide in Christ. Struggling with temperance? Abide in Christ. Don't have joy? Abide in Christ. This must be our focus; not doing works, but abiding in Christ. As we abide, the fruit of His life within us will manifest automatically and we are assured to bear much fruit. Remember what Jesus said, *"Without me you can do nothing."*

Let me tell you something friends. Get as far away as you possibly can from those telling you that you do not need the baptism of the Holy Ghost.

The impartation of the Holy Ghost is the power of God which engrafts you into the vine when you are born again. After you are born again, you need to be filled with the Holy Ghost (which is what it means to be baptized), to be provided sustenance for your spiritual life as He gives you the mind of Christ and the power to walk out your faith.

What we are missing in this present Church Age is the discipline necessary to walk with God. Jesus didn't come to make church members. He came to make disciples, meaning those who are disciplined under His word. Living in Christ means living in His word and making the word the very essence and source of your life. God is not looking for us to feel anything about His word or to put our take on it. He is looking for us to obey it. Those who follow Christ obey Him no matter what and understand that persecution is a part of their stake in this life.

The modern day Christian is offended because they don't have a Coke to drink or because they have a hangnail. We've become soft and tender, too educated and too bright for our own good. It is time for us to return to the realities of the Bible and the faithfulness necessary to walk with Jesus Christ daily. We must return to the basic disciplines of prayer, fasting, and worship, along with detailed and intricate Bible study to understand exactly what we have entered into as children of God.

It is truly ridiculous how many professing Christians have no knowledge of the Bible. They accept at face value whatever is told to them from the pulpit with no questions asked because they don't have their own personal study time. There is no discipline in prayer or seeking the revelation of God as presented through His Son, Jesus Christ. You must abide in the vine, live in the vine, and stay in the vine. You must meditate on the word of God day and night, night and day, until it transforms your mind to think like God and not like yourself.

Don't let the devices of the enemy choke off the life God is growing within you. You must abide in the vine and let the sap in that vine recreate a new you in order for your fruit to remain. This will produce the freedom you've been searching for all your life. Millions of Christians are talking to psychologists, counselors, and anyone who says they can provide the answers for life's problems. Let me assure you that no answers exist on the physical plane. The only answer is organically reproducing Christ inside of you; such is our only hope of glory.

This page intentionally left blank.

Chapter 5 - Break Up Your Fallow Ground

Transformance vs. Performance

> *Jeremiah 4:3-4*
> *For thus saith the LORD to the men of Judah and Jerusalem,*
> *Break up your fallow ground, and sow not among thorns.*
> *Circumcise yourselves to the LORD, and take away the*
> *foreskins of your heart, ye men of Judah and inhabitants*
> *of Jerusalem: lest my fury come forth like fire, and burn*
> *that none can quench it, because of the evil of your doings.*

Before salvation, we were filthy, unregenerate sinners whose thoughts and ways were opposed to God. We were alienated from the life of God in our minds because we loved the things of this world. We were His enemies (Romans 5:10). Being led by our carnal appetites, we refused the discipline of God and went about doing whatever we desired to do. Yet we did not understand that our spiritual life is organic. Whatsoever we sow, we will reap; whether unto righteousness or unrighteousness (Psalm 7:14; Galatians 6:7-8). As we began to suffer the consequences of sin - a chaotic mind, fear, hatred, abuse, rejection, debauchery, etc. - we finally cried out to God for His divine intervention. In mercy He provided it, birthing us anew by the power of His Holy Spirit so that we may be saved.

This is when the battle begins. Galatians 5:17 states, *"For the flesh lusteth against the Spirit, and the Spirit against the flesh: and these are **contrary the one to the other**: so that ye cannot do the things that ye would."* The flesh and the Spirit represent two types of life which are contrary to each other. After the salvation process is wrought, a war breaks out in the soul of man as his flesh - the old nature - seeks to live. It contends with the new life we have been given in the spirit because it does not want to die! Yet the death of that old nature must occur for the new nature birthed by God to come forth. Remember, one nature can only live at the expense of the other.

This is why, after salvation, so many Christians stop abiding in the One who saved them and instead turn aside to the works of the flesh. You see, the flesh wants to live. It will not surrender willingly to its own death and engaging in war against it does not always feel good. In regards to this struggle, the Apostle Paul writes:

> *1 Corinthians 9:27*
> *But **I keep under** my body, and bring it into **subjection**:*

lest that by any means, when I have preached to others, I myself should be a castaway.

Paul speaks of salvation here as the running of a race. In order to win this race, he states that he must "keep under" his body (the flesh), and bring it into "subjection".

The Greek word for the phrase "keep under" in this text is *hypopiazo* which literally means to "**beat black and blue**". It is to hit something hard enough so that it leaves bruises; to give something intolerable annoyances and to discipline it through hardships. The Greek word for "subjection" is *doulagogeo* which means to "lead away into slavery".

My friends, this is not a passive or light war. You cannot be apathetic. This is why God has called you to be a soldier (2 Timothy 2:3-4). We must be able to endure hardness as a good soldier so that the life of Christ can come to maturity within us. The flesh is fighting for its life and if you do not engage it, it **will** overtake you and snuff out the new life God has planted within. As Paul stated, left to its own devices, the flesh will make you a castaway.

To save its life, the flesh may even hide in plain sight by resorting to religious works, doing its best to simulate and emulate the life imparted by God. However, even religious works of the flesh are still dead works. It is still the flesh at work. It is still carnal, but now it is masquerading under a religious veneer; attempting to earn God's favor in its own effort versus obedience to God's word. What is the result of not crucifying the flesh? We go looking for some man or organization to give us rules to live by; things we can do to be righteous. We fool ourselves into believing that adherence to that entity means we will be accepted by God. We no longer need to study to show ourselves approved, we can simply come to church and hear the word from the man of God. What they say becomes law, and we are absolved of any personal accountability before the Lord (so we think). Most of all, the flesh still gets to live because the truth about the organic nature of the Gospel and the need to crucify the flesh is not preached. The Bible tells us that there will come a time when men will no longer endure sound doctrine, but after their own lusts will seek teachers with itching ears based upon their own lusts. This is happening all around us and has been the downfall of millions of people over the centuries as the old man goes looking for a priest, pastor, or Moses to take the place of Jesus in their lives.

However, there is no other name given amongst men whereby we must be saved (Acts 4:12). That name is Jesus Christ, the Son of God. There is no other hope for salvation. Any other religious figure leads to damnation. You cannot trust in denominations. God will never downgrade His plan or His disciplines to fit the desires of men. Simply stated friends, you and I must change for us to walk with God. That change takes place as you abide in the vine; as you live in Christ, the word of God becomes your only source of life.

The reason people are able to sit up in make believe churches such as World Changers, The Potter's House, Kenneth Hagin Ministries, etc. is because of the nature they possess. Once God has changed your nature, the appetite for delusions will drop out of you. Keep the old nature, and the delusion will remain appealing. This is why there's no way to save a person who wants to be deceived; the nature in them desires the deception. Only an organically born again child of God can come out from amongst them and touch not the unclean thing (2 Corinthians 6:17). For God to receive you to Himself as His child, you **must** be a partaker of the divine nature.

The only qualification for Heaven is that you have been born again to reflect the nature of Jesus Christ. You don't go to Heaven because of what you do or what you don't do. As shocking as it may seem, you don't even go to Hell because of what you do or don't do. You go to Heaven or Hell because of what you are. Your nature dictates your actions; actions don't dictate your nature. For example, a liar tells lies. However, a liar who is not currently telling a lie is still a liar. You can stop the actions, but that alone will not change what you really are. You can be a liar who is not lying, a drunk who's not drinking, a smoker who's not smoking, and so on. This is why you must be changed on the **inside**. You must be transformed by having your mind renewed.

You can put the Devil in Hell for a million years, and he'll still come out of it as the Devil. You can put one of his followers in there with him and they'll still come out of it following Satan. Not even punishment can change your nature. There have been people who have gone to jail, only to come out and commit the same crime again. The jail time didn't get rid of the criminal mindset. So friends, you had better understand this. If you don't get to that cross and mortify that old nature, you will be lost because there is a delusion tailor made for the nature you possess. There must be a nature coming from above through organic growth which qualifies you for Heaven.

Make no mistake about it. Not your race, gender, education, finances, or any other worldly standard matters. The Gospel excludes only one type of individual: Adam and those who are of his lineage. You must understand that this thing is a battle of two natures. God Himself said, *"Jacob have I loved, but Esau have I hated."* (Romans 9:13). God hated the **nature** that Esau possessed. Esau sold his whole birthright for a bowl of pottage - food and materials on the temporal earthly plane meant more to him than the things of God (Genesis 25:34). He counted the birthright as worthless in order to acquire more for himself in the here and now. That same spirit is alive today, deceiving hundreds of thousands globally.

Salvation is simply the killing of the nature which had you bound to sin and the birthing of the nature of Jesus Christ within you. As the one dies and the other matures, you are changed into the image of the One conceived within you. I know many of you who read this book may struggle with this because the nature in you is being reinforced by demonic entities to make sure you don't get free. Yet, my prayer for you as you read this book is that the power of God come upon you and shackle that fallen nature to hold it at bay. That way, your mind can clearly understand and perceive the truths God has revealed in His Scriptures.

Jesus has chosen and ordained us to bring forth much fruit. This fruit should remain, not start dying on the vine. That way, whatsoever we ask of the Father in His name, believing, He will give it to us. We are to abide in the vine so that our minds are transformed to reflect the mind of Jesus Christ. The key to prayer is that we are not to pray, think, and ask based upon our own minds. Rather, we pray with the mind of Christ, who already knows what God desires for us. This way, we know that we are praying in line with God's will because the mind of God through Jesus Christ via His Spirit has been imparted in us. That is the goal; for us to be transformed by the renewing of the mind so that we can prove what is that good, acceptable, and perfect will of God. This happens as a result of abiding in the vine. My mind will be transformed and I will be able to hear from God and perform His will in these last days. As the end of the world approaches us, my counsel to you is to be found abiding in the vine.

Your Fruit Should Remain

You cannot afford to drift off now. If you have ever studied your Bible, study it more now. Pray and seek God for the revelation of His word because we are entering into dangerous and treacherous times. There are many delusions and schemes cooked up by the Devil to destroy you. Knowing God now is not an option. It is a very definite necessity.

As we enter into these last of the last days, the Bible speaks of the strong delusions that will be coming our way. The Apostle Paul warns of how they will begin to take hold of the apostate church.

> *1 Timothy 4:1-5*
> *Now the Spirit speaketh expressly, that in the latter times some shall depart from the faith, giving heed to **seducing spirits and doctrines of devils**. Speaking lies in hypocrisy; having their conscience seared with a hot iron; forbidding to marry, and commanding to abstain from meats, which*

God hath created to be received with thanksgiving of them which believe and know the truth. For every creature of God is good, and nothing to be refused, if it be received with thanksgiving: for it is sanctified by the word of God and prayer.

Notice that these doctrines are preached by demons. Satan is adept at setting up his ministers as ministers of righteousness (2 Corinthians 11:14-15). This is why we need to be like the Bereans, studying God's word for ourselves to see if the things we are being taught are true (Acts 17:11).

Beware when people begin to tell you what you can and cannot eat. The text here clearly says that every creature of God is good and nothing to be refused if received with thanksgiving. Does that mean everything you eat is good for you? No, we must still use wisdom. However, it does mean that there are no religious doctrines around what you eat except for what is outlined in the book of Acts.

Acts 15:28-29
For it seemed good to the Holy Ghost, and to us, to lay upon you no greater burden than these necessary things; That ye abstain from meats offered to idols, and from blood, and from things strangled, and from fornication: from which if ye keep yourselves, ye shall do well. Fare ye well.

The Church at Antioch told the Gentiles not to ingest blood because the blood contained the filth and diseases of the animals they were eating. To make it fit for consumption, the blood had to be poured out of the animal before ingestion. This is also why they were instructed not to eat things strangled, as that forced the blood to remain in the animal. Yet, many have taken this simple and sensible instruction and used it to try and bind people under a law. It is this type of mindset which has resulted in a churchworld with seemingly more laws than Moses presented from Mount Sinai. How is it possible for us to have gotten this far away from being led by the Holy Spirit of God to turning ourselves to laws, rules, and regulations again? Who has bewitched the church?

It is simple; the problem is the carnal mind. The carnal mind is not subject to the word of God neither can it be (Romans 8:7). A carnal mind even fights against the mind of Christ being developed within you so that you do not become spiritual (1 Corinthians 9:11). The result is that you will by nature stumble around in darkness and put yourself under bondage, becoming a slave to some man or woman's personality. This will lead you down the road of destruction and cut off your growth in God. **All** of Satan's weapons are designed to stop your organic growth.

The only threat you present to Satan is that you might just become a self-contained, organically-grown son of God who manifests the life of Jesus Christ. Every demonic attack aims to keep you in the flesh, trying to appease organizational structures, men's personalities, and your own conscience. The Scripture says that if we seek to be a pleaser of men then we cannot be the servant of Christ (Galatians 1:10). At some point, don't you get tired of trying to perform for man? Wouldn't you rather walk with God as a son, knowing the peace that surpasses all understanding because the wall of separation between you and God has been removed? If so, then you must get on with the task of nurturing the new life that is within you.

Tend to the garden, the husbandry, that is within you. Let Christ grow to maturity and God will have nothing against you. There is no condemnation to those who walk not according to the flesh, but after the Spirit (Romans 8:1). God has done something so tremendous and unbelievable, that most of us have a hard time believing it can be this simple. The Gospel is organic. As you abide in Him - putting your whole life in His hands - you will see the promises of God come to pass. God is not interested in what you do. He's interested in changing what you are. Doesn't common sense dictate that if you change who a man is, you will automatically change what he does? On the other hand, you can change what you do and never change who you really are.

God will let you stumble around the Wilderness of Sin just as He did with Israel until you finally give up and say:

> "Lord, take my life over and lead me into the Promised Land. Fill me with the Holy Ghost and guide me into all truth. I'm tired of looking for answers to all of these addictions: pornography, alcohol, illicit sex, drugs, gambling, etc. I can no longer deal with the problems of my spouse, my kids, my job. I'm tired of trying to live up to other peoples standards with all of the rejection, hurt, pain, and fear that comes along with it. I'm sick of sickness and disease; I'm almost sick of living. God, please take my life over!"

Isn't it plain to see that it has been an utter failure trying to live your life the way you saw fit? Left to our own devices, we wind up shipwrecked, crazy, and almost ready to commit suicide, so why continue on in this agony? That is exactly what it is. It is agony to try and serve God through the dictates of religion while having no life from God inside. God only knows the guilt, shame, and agony many reading this book bear, trying to carry the weight of religion while still ensnared to the sin which so easily besets you (Hebrews 12:1). Even in reading this book, the urge to enter into the dark world of pornography is eating away at many of you. You've tried everything; prayed, fasted, sought God, but still the addictions remain. No matter how it looks on the outside, still the flesh holds on for dear life. Sin is not an action, but a nature that must be crucified.

Extermination

Romans 7:1-25
Know ye not, brethren, (for I speak to them that know the law,) how that the law hath dominion over a man as long as he liveth? For the woman which hath an husband is bound by the law to her husband so long as he liveth; but if the husband be dead, she is loosed from the law of her husband. So then if, while her husband liveth, she be married to another man, she shall be called an adulteress: but if her husband be dead, she is free from that law; so that she is no adulteress, though she be married to another man. Wherefore, my brethren, ye also are become dead to the law by the body of Christ; that ye should be married to another, even to him who is raised from the dead, that we should bring forth fruit unto God. For when we were in the flesh, the motions of sins, which were by the law, did work in our members to bring forth fruit unto death. But now we are delivered from the law, that being dead wherein we were held; that we should serve in newness of spirit, and not in the oldness of the letter. What shall we say then? Is the law sin? God forbid. Nay, I had not known sin, but by the law: for I had not known lust, except the law had said, Thou shalt not covet. But sin, taking occasion by the commandment, wrought in me all manner of concupiscence. For without the law sin was dead. For I was alive without the law once: but when the commandment came, sin revived, and I died. And the commandment, which was ordained to life, I found to be unto death. For sin, taking occasion by the commandment, deceived me, and by it slew me. Wherefore the law is holy, and the commandment holy, and just, and good. Was then that which is good made death unto me? God forbid. But sin, that it might appear sin, working death in me by that

*which is good; that sin by the commandment might become
exceeding sinful. For we know that the law is spiritual: but
I am carnal, sold under sin. For that which I do I allow not:
for what I would, that do I not; but what I hate, that do I.
If then I do that which I would not, I consent unto the law
that it is good. Now then it is no more I that do it, but sin
that dwelleth in me. For I know that in me (that is, in my
flesh,) dwelleth no good thing: for to will is present with
me; but how to perform that which is good I find not. For
the good that I would I do not: but the evil which I would
not, that I do. Now if I do that I would not, it is no more
I that do it, but sin that dwelleth in me. I find then a law,
that, when I would do good, evil is present with me. For I
delight in the law of God after the inward man: but I see
another law in my members, warring against the law of
my mind, and bringing me into captivity to the law of sin
which is in my members. O wretched man that I am! Who
shall deliver me from the body of this death? I thank God
through Jesus Christ our Lord. So then with the mind I
myself serve the law of God; but with the flesh the law of sin.*

In this text, Paul speaks of the sin nature being at war with the spirit man inside of him. As evidence of this war, Paul says that the things he wants to do he cannot, and the things he does not want to do, he does. He consents that the problem is not with the law, but with him because sin lives in him. Sin is not inanimate. Scripture depicts sin as a living entity (Genesis 4:7). Sin is a living nature which must be crucified and put to death in order for you to be free.

The bondage you are under is not one of actions, desires, and feelings. Those are the things which keep psychologists and psychiatrists analyzing a situation forever, but unable to arrive at a resolution because sin is a nature. You can talk about homosexuality, lesbianism, child abuse, pornography, and other addictions from now until Hell freezes over, but that still won't get rid of it. The flesh must be put to death. The only place it will find peace is in its resting place on the cross.

Remember, the Apostle Paul did not say that Jesus Christ was crucified for us. We were crucified with Him to the extent that it is not even we who live anymore, but Christ lives within us (Galatians 2:20). That's a significant, powerful change brothers and sisters, because it releases us from the curse of the law - the curse of sin and death. It is freedom found in the only place where you find freedom: in a graveyard. I guarantee you, everyone in a graveyard is free from the bondages of sin. He who is dead is freed from sin (Romans 6:7). You become free from sin through Jesus Christ's death because He took you to the cross *with Him* to kill the nature that enslaved you.

Now I know what most of you are thinking right now, "If that be true, then why do I still undergo this torment from the sin nature? If Jesus Christ has set me free from it, then why am I still agonizing trying to get rid of it?" Look again at Romans Chapter 7. Paul was going through the **same thing** until he realized one thing: his escape was found in Jesus Christ. The escape was found in meditating on God's word day and night. It was found through prayer and fasting. The escape was found by putting to death that old nature which is being stimulated by the world.

You see friends, the reason we were so filthy, defiled, and contaminated is because that is the condition of the world. As long as we have an appetite for the world, it will breathe its decaying life into and empower the fallen, Adamic nature. The stimulus for the life of the flesh is a love of the world (1 John 2:15).

Consider a person who is brain dead and lying in a hospital bed. If you go inside the room, there will be all kinds of gizmos attached to the person. You may even ask, "Is he still alive?" The response would be, "No, he is actually brain dead, but we're keeping him alive through artificial life-support. Once we cut-off the machines, he will die." This is what we face in our walk with God. The Adamic nature was crucified on the cross. This is why Jesus is referred to as the last Adam (1 Corinthians 15:45). Yet, this nature still has all looks and appearances of being alive! It has desires, thoughts, preferences, etc. You can **feel** its inputs all in your members. That is because interaction with, and attachment to, the world simulates the life of the old man.

It is just like Frankenstein's monster. Frankenstein put together a bunch of dead body parts, shot the monster full of electricity, and the next thing you know, it was walking around like a natural man. He had been artificially raised from the dead. It is the same way with the old Adamic nature. As long as you feed him, he will keep on ambulating around the Earth as if he never died. Further, he'll plague you all of your life until you are through with him. As the saying goes, "Be killing sin or sin will be killing you."

Philippians 3:17-21
Brethren, be followers together of me, and mark them which walk so as ye have us for an ensample. (For many walk, of whom I have told you often, and now tell you even weeping, that they are the enemies of the cross of Christ: whose end is destruction, whose God is their belly, and whose

glory is in their shame, who mind earthly things.) For our conversation is in heaven; from whence also we look for the Saviour, the Lord Jesus Christ: who shall change our vile body, that it may be fashioned like unto his glorious body, according to the working whereby he is able even to subdue all things unto himself.

Here the Apostle Paul expresses the importance of the cross in the life of a believer. He says that many are walking in a way that makes them the enemy of the cross. They come up with devices to stop you and me from getting on that cross. These men are headed for destruction and they worship their own bellies. In other words, they serve their own appetites and like to indulge the lusts of their flesh. They are greedy, gluttonous, and covetous. They try to heap up earthly things for themselves while glorying in that which should cause them shame. On the contrary, our life is to come from Heaven as we are waiting for Jesus to come and change our vile bodies to be like His glorious body.

Let me tell you something. If you believe that most of these present-day doctrines are from God, then you had better think again. Men like Leroy Thompson are preaching "Money Cometh". Creflo Dollar preaches prosperity. T. D. Jakes uses emotional gimmickry to get you worked up in the flesh. John Avanzini and Oral Roberts taught that Jesus was rich. These are all masters of illusion. They are given over to Satan for the purpose of catching you in a snare. Unless the carnal nature has been put to death in you, then you will fall prey to a delusion. Jesus says the deception will be so strong that, if it were possible, even the very elect would be deceived (Matthew 24:24).

Enemies of the cross don't want the sin nature put to death because they are using the sin nature to live off of you. In order for their plan to work, they must stop you from getting on the cross. These false prophets and preachers have found a way to get rich off of people who don't know the Bible and are still bound by sin. In this, they ensure that those who follow them will be damned to Hell.

I'm not trying to anger you with my words. I am just presenting simple Gospel truths to basically shake you into reality and wake you up out of this sleepiness so that God can give you light. Paul is warning us in Philippians that as long as a man can hold that cross back from you, he can keep you under his spell forever. Too many Christians have been bewitched because they had a nature that gave an open door to a preacher who is really a sorcerer. The new birth began as a work of the Spirit, so what makes us think that we can now finish the work of being perfected in the flesh (Galatians 3:3)? Do not go back to the flesh! The cross is our freedom. My crucifixion ends my struggle with the nature which has been cursing me my whole life.

Have you made the cross your enemy, seeing it as an expression of death which must be avoided at all cost? Do you see Jesus on the cross for you or do you see yourself on the cross with Him? This perspective will make all the difference in the world for your life. A lot of supposedly well-meaning Christians tell people to bring themselves to the foot of the cross and be saved. While that sounds and feels good, and even seems very religious, that is not the truth of the Gospel.

Friends, you don't come to the foot of the cross to be saved. You must get **on that cross** and leave this world behind to be saved. I make no appeals to your culture, color, age, or any other characteristic of your flesh. The cross can kill anybody. It will mortify you and me. In so doing, it will eradicate the decaying, filthy nature of flesh - and all the ways that has kept you in bondage - so that Christ might live.

Don't you want to be free for real? Aren't you tired of hypocriting around? Sitting in church lusting after the pastor, the piano player, the deacon, the young girls in the choir? At some point you have to decide that you want to be free for you! You have to turn yourself completely over to God. At some point, the kids must realize that there is more to life than the Hip Hop generation along with the music and entertainment which feeds the old nature. It is time for somebody - anybody - to proclaim that this is the way and follow it: sanctification unto holiness (Isaiah 30:21). You must walk in sanctification in order to crucify the old man so that the new man can live.

Why put off your own liberty? The cross is the way of escape. It ends my agony. Once you know this, the cross becomes your friend and something beautiful in your life. Make it the desire of your heart as a doorway for eternal life. Paul says that the lying hypocritical preachers make the cross their enemy, and yours. In these last days, God must raise up a people who will see the cross as a drawing mechanism in order to be freed from the anarchy of this life. Why choose the filth of this world over being dedicated and consecrated to God through the cross? This is the sacrifice we must make in order to be raised from the dead as a living epistle read of all men to and for the glory of God (Romans 12:1).

He that is dead is freed from sin. Are you dead? Are you free from the bondage of sin? Remember, sin is a nature, and each nature reproduces after its own kind. When it does reproduce, it will carry with it the actions which testify to its nature.

Is the cross your enemy or is it your doorway to freedom? You must choose.

Cultivation

In order to keep the flesh crucified, we must stop feeding it and instead feed our spirits. Remember, you are what you eat. Whatever life you feed upon will be what grows within and manifests from you. As long as we keep our minds, eyes, ears, emotions, thoughts and every part of our being engaged in the world, the crucified nature from Adam will be bolstered by artificial life support. It will receive impulses to keep that nature walking around and living while he should be on a cross dead. Just as a husbandman regularly prunes a plant in order to improve its overall health and fruitfulness, so do we need to cut out that which would choke off the new life in us. The more we cut, the more fruitful we will become. You have to grow one life and starve the other.

Think about it this way. Hugh Hefner could never have built an empire based upon naked women and hedonism if it were not for the appetites of those who support this perversion. The industry knows that if you lose that appetite, then you will have no propensity to buy their products. So you understand then that the most important quest for the publishers of Playboy is to make sure that your appetite never goes away. It is the same with all inordinate affections; food, drugs, music, TV, movies, or whatever binds you. Cut off the stimuli and the appetite will die. Yet Satan is banking on the fact that you don't want to cut out the stimuli. Why? Because he knows that it feels good. Sexual sin, overeating, getting drunk or high...these things all feel good to the flesh.

The Devil's ingenious trap, his masterful stroke with sin, is that he puts his filth, decadence, and destruction in attractive environments that are pleasurable to the flesh. Anybody knows that when you go into the forest to trap an animal, you are not going to bait the trap with something the animal hates. You bait the trap with something the animal will find irresistible. The Devil works the same way. He is going to draw you according to the lusts of your own flesh, not with something you hate (James 1:14-16). Knowing your weakness, he will come again and again to see if you will give in to temptation. Believe me, the Devil has a plan to exploit everything in us which is like him.

Unless you are trying to put forth a phony and hypocritical appearance, then you know that there was a lot wrong with you when you got saved. To tell the truth, there are likely still things wrong with you today. That is just being honest. This is why God wants to systematically work out of you all that is undermining your relationship with Him. Salvation is a process. Don't let anybody kid you. It is not a one-time profession of faith. You enter into an organic process when you come to Jesus Christ.

Break Up Your Fallow Ground

The goal of God is not to push people away from Him or make it difficult to be reconciled to Him. He is trying to draw people near into an intimate relationship, but sin is in the way. The Lord says clearly that our sins have separated us from Him (Isaiah 59:2). God is not a sinner, so the problem could not be with Him. By default, the problem must be us. Since God cannot have fellowship with sin, He seeks to purge and remove sin from us so that we can fellowship with Him (Ephesians 5:1-6; I Peter 2:11). That is what the Christian race is all about.

In these last days, our faith in Christ must become more than just words; it must become our very lives (I Corinthians 2:4). The nature and essence of the life of God was flowing through Paul because he knew his life was to be a sacrifice. Therefore, Paul did not allow himself to live as a citizen of this world. He did not share in the hedonistic, self-gratifying, self-appeasing mindset of the world. Instead, Paul accepted that his life was one of austerity and discipline so that he might bring the Gospel to the lost and manifest the nature of love by the power of God working through him.

It is time to put yourself to death now, so that you don't fall later. I am sure we can ask David about Bathsheba, Samson about Delilah, or Solomon about all of the many women he had. Any appetite which is not crucified will lead to your destruction. Thousands of believers have been destroyed by their own unrestrained lust.

We cannot continue in the agonizing duality of trying to live two lives - the flesh and the spiritual. There are two natures at war, and one of them has to be mortified. One of them must go to the cross to be crucified. Which one will it be? In order to walk with God, the flesh must be mortified. We are to abide in the vine until the Adamic nature is put to death and the nature of Christ takes us over.

Remember this. One of the most frightening truths that you will ever be told is that if you do not crucify the Adamic nature in you, rest assured that the Adamic nature in you will crucify Christ (Hebrews 6:6). At that point, all you have to look forward to is a fiery indignation and destruction in Hell. This is nothing to kid ourselves about, friends. Jesus' promise is that He will reward those who overcome that nature. To do that we must abide in the vine and cut off those things which make us unfruitful. We must stay with Him. We must stay faithful. We must meditate on, read, and ingest His word. We must desire His word like it is pure, precious gold (Proverbs 3:13-14). In times like these, the only thing that can sustain us is life in the vine.

This page intentionally left blank.

Chapter 6 - Transplanted for New Life

New Soil

> *Hebrews 11:8-10, 14-16*
> *By faith Abraham, when he was called to **go out into a***
> ***place which he should after receive for an inheritance**,*
> *obeyed; and he went out, not knowing whither he went. By*
> *faith he sojourned in the land of promise, as in a strange*
> *country, dwelling in tabernacles with Isaac and Jacob,*
> *the heirs with him of the same promise: For he looked for*
> *a city which hath foundations, whose builder and maker*
> *is God...For they that say such things declare plainly that*
> *they seek a country. And truly, if they had been mindful of*
> *that country from whence they came out, they might have*
> *had opportunity to have returned. **But now they desire a***
> ***better country, that is, an heavenly:** wherefore God is not*
> *ashamed to be called their God: for he hath prepared for*
> *them a city.*

We discussed previously how the nutrients needed to support the life of the vine comes from the soil. In order for us to abide in the vine - which is Jesus Christ - we must be rooted in a life source that is *different* from what we were used to in the world. We must be fed from a different type of soil, as Jesus was. For this to happen, we must go on an exodus.

> *John 8:23*
> *And he said unto them, Ye are from beneath; I am from*
> *above: ye are of this world; I am not of this world.*

The entire journey into Christ is a spiritual exodus. Forget about all of the dictates in religion about what you have to do or not do. It's not about performance and trying to keep all these laws, rules, and regulations in the letter. Salvation is a moving of the people, an exodus.

An exodus is a mass departure or immigration. It is everyone loading up all of our belongings, leaving this place behind, and going to a completely new location to settle there. The Bible itself is logically written to reveal the story of an exodus; a journey from captivity to freedom. Looking at the physical exodus when Moses led Israel out of Egypt gives us more understanding about what we are undergoing in our spiritual exodus into Christ.

The Organic Gospel

Israel began to sojourn in Egypt during a famine and stayed there for 430 years. God, being Omniscient, had sent Joseph into Egypt years before in preparation for that time. Although Joseph faced all kinds of trials and tribulations, he was ultimately lifted up to become the second most powerful man in Egypt. However after Joseph's passing, Israel began to lose favor with Egypt. The Hebrews were foreigners and didn't serve the same gods as the Egyptians. As Israel became a great nation, Egypt perceived them as a threat and enslaved them as a means of maintaining control. From their captivity, Israel cried out to God for release and His answer was to take them on an exodus.

Understand that this is also a reflection of the Church. In the Bible, Egypt is a picture of the world. The Body of Christ is under the oppression of the world's systems while God is growing His church. Just as the Hebrews were in Egypt, we are strangers in this world; this is not our home. We don't serve the same gods as they do, and as a result, they don't like us. Everything in the world is designed to restrain the people of God so that they do not walk in God's promises. To be freed from the world's oppression, we too must go on an exodus.

Every step in Israel's exodus was centered around them giving up something. It is the same for us. In order to move forward, you have got to let go of something in the past, or even something in the present. Think about it logically. You cannot move to Asia while holding on to the United States. You cannot even get to the fourth grade and hold on to the third grade. With every step of progression you have to give up something if you want to keep moving forward. The first thing that Israel was called upon to leave behind in their exodus was their affinity for Egypt.

Now consider this. What would have been so hard about leaving Egypt? The Egyptians had ensnared the Israelites in slavery; they were a people in bondage (Exodus 20:2). The Egyptians had demeaned their men, abused their women, and murdered their children. Who wouldn't want to leave that? Yet, the Israelites didn't have a hard time leaving the reality of their situation in Egypt; they had a hard time parting with their imaginations about, and lusts for, Egypt. Their own lusts for the things the Egyptians had kept them tied and bound to that which enslaved them (2 Corinthians 2:5).

God separated Israel from Egypt physically when they crossed the Red Sea, drowning Pharaoh and his armies. Yet, there was damage done to the soul of the Israelites which had to be dealt with as well. The enemy was now **within them** because years spent in slavery had caused them to exalt Egypt as the standard and seek Egypt's approval. Worship of anything causes your soul to be conformed inwardly into the image of what is worshipped. Therefore, their own idolatry of Egypt led them to esteem the worldly riches of Egypt as the standard for success in life. The lust for those things allowed them to be bewitched by the sorcery of Egypt's false religious system.

As with the Hebrews, the problem with many professing Christians is that they don't want to let go of the world because they still lust after the things in it. Instead of having crucified the flesh and its lusts, they hold on with both hands to that which is yoking them to the world and keeping them in the house of bondage. When your entire being is focused on holding onto and sustaining your life down here, you are an Egyptian. You are bound by Egyptian thinking and living in the earth as a slave.

At some point, aren't you better off dead than as a slave? We can see the results of this bondage all around us as people fall for Satan's false depictions of success. They strive with each other to get along with, and court the favor of, the world. They judge themselves and others based upon how many worldly goods they possess. Their own idolatry blinds them because looks can be deceiving. The material goods a person has does not tell you what is happening on the inside of a person. This is why we need the Holy Ghost. We will never be able to see our own true condition, let alone the condition of others, in judging by appearances (John 7:24). We need to go on an exodus so that we can have eyes to see what is really going on spiritually.

When Moses confronted Pharaoh with God's command to, *"Let my people go!"* Pharaoh refused to do it. Instead, Pharaoh called upon the magicians Jannes and Jambres to mimic the miracles Moses performed. The Egyptians were able to match these supernatural displays until Moses finally did something that they could not duplicate. Yet, the supernatural signs God demonstrated through Moses were not only for the Egyptians' sake; it was to remind Israel that the Lord God is Sovereign and more than able to deliver them (Exodus 4:2-9). God needed to turn their hearts back to Him again, and to do this, He had to confront the divinations which held them captive. It is the same for us today.

The god of this world is the father of lies. He uses fantasy and sorcery in order to keep your mind engaged in his kingdom, which is centered in time and space. In our spiritual exodus, God is moving us out of time and space into eternity - from a focus on things in the physical realm to the spiritual realm - so as to free us from captivity to the enemy (Colossians 3:2). He systematically reveals to us those things in this world which are keeping us from progressing into the realm of the spirit where He is. If you are a real Christian, that is what you are trying to do. Your whole life is centrally focused on getting rid of a time and space mentality.

Look at what's coming upon the world. You can see the debauchery and decay as the whole world is corrupting. Why are we holding onto this? We need to embark on an exodus. Repent! Say, "God I see it. This is my problem and I am sorry. I'm ready to change right now. Whatever I have to do to get it right, I'll make amends for it." God will send you to people to rectify situations where you said or did something wrong. He says that if you have anything against another, forgive them so that your Father in heaven might forgive you (Mark 11:25). You cannot hold onto some kind of grudge and expect God to bless you. Neither can you hold on to anything from the world, as doing so will leave you outside of the camp (Joshua 7:1-26). The Church is moving away from this time and space arena into the spiritual things of God. Everything which is in the world - the lust of the flesh, the lust of the eyes, and the pride of life - is **not** of the Father and must be left behind as you proceed on this exodus into new life (1 John 2:16).

The Axe is Laid to the Root

> *Exodus 23:23*
> *For mine Angel shall go before thee, and bring thee in unto the Amorites, and the Hittites, and the Perizzites, and the Canaanites, the Hivites, and the Jebusites: and I will cut them off.*

In the Old Testament, God's people had to war against foreign tribes in a physical Promised Land. In the New Testament, God's people have to war against demons in a spiritual Promised Land. In the Old Testament, God commanded them to take possession of the land. In the New Testament, God commands us to take possession of our souls. Such is the Promised Land for the Christian; getting to the place where our souls are in subjection to our spirits so that we may be led by the Spirit of God and no longer by the carnal inputs from our flesh. It is in that place where we inherit the promises of God.

Now that they were brought out of Egypt, Israel had to wage a war in order to inherit the Promised Land. This required God to deal with the covenant of death they had entered into through their idolatry of Egypt, along with the curses which accompanied that covenant.

You need to know that curses are real. If you can make it through Exodus, Leviticus, Numbers, Deuteronomy, etc. and not see curses, then I don't know what to tell you. Proverbs says that a curse shall not causeless come (Proverbs 26:2). Interspersed in the midst of all sin are the curses that come with sin. You can't figure out why your life won't get right? Why there is always a glass ceiling cutting off your potential? Why it seems like everything you try fails? Why there are a cycle of barren wombs, diseases, infirmity, mental incapacitation, and all kinds of generational problems in your family? You can go on and on dealing with curses, but curses have a cause.

For example, God says to honor your mother and father. Yet many are cursed right now because they have unforgiveness in their hearts against their parents. The unforgiveness anchors your soul to them because you cannot let go of what they did to you when you were growing up. As a result, your parents become an idol to you, and guess what? If you idolize your mother or father through hatred, you will become just like them. Remember, your soul is designed by God to conform to whatever you worship (Romans 6:16); unforgiveness and hatred are forms of worship. You will not only become like the thing you hate most, your own children will feel about you the same way you feel towards your parents.

A hatred for your parents will keep you alive to the world, but God will set up circumstances to show you the truth of how you really feel. When He does, acknowledge that you hate your mother or father and repent so that He may cleanse the hatred from your soul or you will die that way. "Lord, I see it. I am still bound by this hatred. Purge me with hyssop by the blood of Jesus and wash me. I throw myself on the altar."

Maybe you have tried to forgive, but it just keeps gnawing at you. Even just seeing them irritates you. You might have to undergo some fasting and prayer because this is a stronghold in your life. You keep remembering how your father beat and cursed you. How your mother laid around with all those men who molested you. If you die to hating them, then you are set free for God to live in you more. You just might need to offer yourself up to God in prayer and fasting to overcome that which is stymieing you on this exodus into your liberty. You cannot be in agreement with the enemy and get free. If I am attached to this world - and the world has been assigned to damnation - then its fate is my fate.

Whether they are dead or alive, honor your parents by letting go of what they have done. Cast it into the sea of forgetfulness so that you may be free. The irritation you feel when they say something to you is the evidence that you are still embittered towards them.

Why would you think that your mother and father had the ability to know right from wrong having never been instructed? Sinners sin. Just think of those whom you have hurt in your own life. Why not show the same mercy and grace to them that God has shown towards you because they were ignorant of the devil's devices and had no one to teach them?

You cannot hold on to the dictates of a sinner and make it in. Your own mind will not let you go. You will always be conscious of the old IOUs you have against people. You are binding yourself to them by your unforgiveness and it will prevent you from walking in newness of life. That is why you must go on an exodus by way of repentance and release people so that God can answer the prayers you keep praying. "God save my son, save my daughter, save my children!" Yet God is saying you had better look back and get right with your own parents or else you will relive everything they have done.

In the Old Testament, God told Pharaoh to, "Let my people go!" In the New Testament, God is telling His people to, "Let Pharaoh go!" Don't try to justify your bitterness. Let go of that which binds you and thereby cut yourself loose. Holding on to the world, including your lives in this world, is cursing you. It is time to get free and go on an exodus. Do you want out or do you want to stay in this mess the rest of your life trying to figure out why you are under this perpetual curse? A curse shall not causeless come. Honor your father and your mother.

That is how Jesus bore the curse of sin on Himself. Being crucified on a tree made Him a cursed object (Galatians 3:13). The curse that was supposed to come on us came upon Him. The blood of Jesus Christ accomplishes this, but first this blood has to be applied. Jesus' blood in a basin does neither you nor me any good. You have to get the hyssop as referenced in the Old Testament and apply the blood of the lamb to the lintel of your doorpost (Exodus 12:22-23).

> *Psalm 51:6-7*
> *Behold, thou desirest truth in the inward parts: and in the hidden part thou shalt make me to know wisdom. **Purge me with hyssop**, and I shall be clean: wash me, and I shall be whiter than snow.*

How do we get truth in the inward parts? By being purged with hyssop. Israel used hyssop as a purifier and as a way to cleanse the body from sin (Leviticus 14:1-6; Numbers 19:5-6). Medicinally, hyssop is said to be able to repair and reprogram DNA, the genetic code for our cells. These properties of hyssop get to the heart of what the problem is with fallen man: through sin: man became a *genetically* mutated creation.

The fall of man was genetic. It impacted man's gene pool, DNA, and chromosomes. Sin wasn't just what Adam and Eve did in the Garden of Eden, it is what they became - and so did their seed. You didn't sin by happenstance; you sinned because you had the genetic makeup of a sinner which was passed down from your father, Adam. This is how death was passed to all from Adam (Romans 5:12). Sin is not merely the acts you commit, it is the very nature possessed by those who are not in Christ. We were *by nature* children of wrath (Ephesians 2:3). The sin nature - which the Bible often refers to as the old man - is completely different from the nature God imparted to man at his creation. Adam was called the son of God because He was created in God's image. However, no other human was ever called the son of God again until Jesus came (John 1:12). Why? Because sin so perverted man that he was no longer in the image of the One who created him. He became a mutant whom God could no longer receive as His own. Jesus came in the likeness of *"sinful flesh"* and condemned sin *"in the flesh"* (Romans 8:3). The problem of sin was not merely in our actions, but in the essence of who we were at our core.

This is why the final plague was for the Angel of death to kill the firstborn sons of Egypt. It will, in fact, take nothing less than this to free the church. We must be delivered from the world by having the firstborn male child of the world killed, which is the old man. The axe must be laid to the root of the tree (Matthew 3:10; Luke 3:9). God is not trying to simply get you to stop sinning. His desire is to cut off the root of sin within you, which means killing off the sinful nature. Kill the old man and you will be released from Egypt. As long as the old man lives, you remain captivated by this world. The first born in you has to be sacrificed up so that the spiritual you can leave Egypt behind for good. You will no longer be a slave to Egypt, and Egypt will no longer be an inward snare to you. Jesus said that the prince of this world comes and has **nothing** in Him (John 14:30). If we are Jesus' Body, then there will likewise be nothing of Satan's world in us.

Historically, Jesus Christ died during Passover and He is our Passover Lamb. God's command that Israel not break even one bone of the Passover lamb's body is representative of Christ, for God had prophesied that not one of His bones would be broken (Exodus 12:46; Psalm 34:20; John 19:33). As the Lamb of God, Jesus took the place of the first born (our old man) so that we might be set free through His crucifixion. Jesus came to restore to man the possibility of becoming a child of God once again through regeneration; re-**gene**-ration. Jesus came to address exactly what the problem was between man and God, and that problem is found in man's genes. That is where the fall took place. We needed a transfusion. The blood of Jesus was not randomly chosen by God as a sanctifier for man. We needed another bloodline which was not contaminated by sin.

> *I John 1:6-7*
> *If we say that we have fellowship with him, and walk in darkness, we lie, and do not the truth: But if we walk in the light, as he is in the light, we have fellowship one with another, **and the blood of Jesus Christ his Son cleanseth us from all sin.***

In using hyssop to have the blood of the lamb applied to Israel's doorposts, God is giving a physical representation of regeneration through Jesus Christ whereby we are redeemed and freed from the power of death. For Israel, the Passover signified a separation from Egypt and sanctification unto the Lord. No longer were they to serve Egypt, but they would now serve the Lord. Similarly, our call is to be sanctified from the world so that we may now serve the Lord.

This is the problem with most Christians, including preachers. They do not understand the fall and as a result, they do not see how God is reversing the fall through faith in Jesus Christ. Now you can understand why religious works and performance can never save you. Such things will never change who you are on the inside, on a genetic level. You cannot save yourself by trying to be good because what you need is a new life type; we must be born again (John 3:3-7; 1 Peter 1:22-23). We need another bloodline and that is what the blood of Jesus is all about.

For believers in Jesus, the hyssop used to apply the blood of the Lamb is the word of God. The word of God transfuses us by giving us another nature; another genetic makeup. We literally become a new creature (2 Corinthians 5:17; Galatians 6:15; 1 John 1:7). The washing of water by the word sanctifies and cleanses us (Ephesians 5:26). It is life to us and health to all of our flesh (Proverbs 4:20-22). As we meditate on God's word, the Spirit of God gives life to the seed sown in our hearts. The hyssop of God's word applies the blood of Jesus to us and we become partakers of the divine nature instead of the sin nature.

> *2 Corinthians 3:18*
> *But we all, with open face beholding as in a glass the glory of the Lord, are **changed into the same image from glory to glory, even as by the Spirit of the Lord**.*

It is communion with Jesus which changes us. Jesus said that unless we eat of His flesh and drink His blood, we can have no life in us (John 6:53). In communion, the bread is the body and the wine is the blood. Jesus is the bread of life and we need His daily bread to live. We ingest His body by ingesting His words. His words are spirit and they are life. As we do, God is rewriting us genetically by the Spirit, changing us from what we were into what He is; only then will we inherit the promises of God.

A Pruning

> *Exodus 12:43-48*
> *And the LORD said unto Moses and Aaron, This is the*
> *ordinance of the Passover: There shall no stranger eat*
> *thereof: But every man's servant that is bought for money,*
> *when thou hast circumcised him, then shall he eat thereof.*
> *A foreigner and an hired servant shall not eat thereof. In*
> *one house shall it be eaten; thou shalt not carry forth ought*
> *of the flesh abroad out of the house; neither shall ye break*
> *a bone thereof. All the congregation of Israel shall keep it.*
> *And when a stranger shall sojourn with thee, and will keep*
> *the Passover to the LORD, let all his males be circumcised,*
> *and then let him come near and keep it; and he shall be as*
> *one that is born in the land: for no uncircumcised person*
> *shall eat thereof.*

God had given the sign of circumcision to Abraham and his descendants as a seal of the covenant He made with him (Genesis 17:1-14; Acts 7:8). Yet, this was only after God had commanded Abraham to *"get thee out"* of the land of his birth and go on a journey into a land he knew not, which God would give him as an inheritance. Before God delivered the Israelites out of Egypt through their exodus, He reminded them of this covenant. This ordinance was not just for the Israelites, but also for any stranger who dwelt among them. Anyone who was uncircumcised was to be excluded, not only from the Passover, but from entering into the Promised Land. Such were guilty of breaking the covenant of God.

Circumcision is the cutting off of the foreskin's flesh as an outward sign that one had been dedicated in covenant to the Lord. It set Israel apart from the world and served as a reminder to them that they were not to mix themselves with the world. We know from Scripture that this sign of circumcision symbolized the work God would perform in those who turn in faith to His Son, Jesus (Romans 4:11-12).

> *Romans 2:29*
> *But he is a Jew, which is one inwardly; and circumcision is*
> *that of the heart, in the spirit, and not in the letter; whose*
> *praise is not of men, but of God.*

Circumcision allows the seed in man to come forth unhindered and uncontaminated. This is the result God wants to produce spiritually in man by circumcising our hearts. Out of the heart flows the issues of life (Proverbs 4:23). Through circumcision, God is removing the stony, calloused heart of the old man and giving us a new heart after His own (Ezekiel 36:26; Romans 2:28-29). It signifies the cutting away of **any** identification with the world so that we may serve the True and Living God. With a circumcised heart, we can carry and show forth the life of Christ within us to the world without perverting it. Remember, all of the Scriptures represent God revealing to us the manifestation of organic life. Everything He does is about sowing, nurturing, and growing this life within us so that we may be fruitful in Him.

What does it mean to be uncircumcised? It means to bear the mark of being outside of the camp and out of covenant with the God of Abraham, Isaac, and Jacob. It is to be an idolater. This is why God commands His people to circumcise their hearts (Jeremiah 4:4; James 4:8). You cannot love the world and serve God. You must be circumcised by having every vestige of the world cut off in order to walk in the righteousness of Jesus Christ, which only comes by faith in His finished work on the cross. Once again, we are on an exodus and with every step you take, you are leaving the old things behind.

1 Corinthians 10:1-12

Moreover, brethren, I would not that ye should be ignorant, how that all our fathers were under the cloud, and all passed through the sea; And were all baptized unto Moses in the cloud and in the sea; And did all eat the same spiritual meat; And did all drink the same spiritual drink: for they drank of that spiritual Rock that followed them: and that Rock was Christ.

*But with many of them God was not well pleased: **for they were overthrown in the wilderness. Now these things were our examples**, to the intent we should not lust after evil things, as they also lusted.*

*Neither be ye idolaters, as were some of them; as it is written, The people sat down to eat and drink, and rose up to play. Neither let us commit fornication, as some of them committed, and fell in one day three and twenty thousand. Neither let us tempt Christ, as some of them also tempted, and were destroyed of serpents. Neither murmur ye, as some of them also murmured, and were destroyed of the destroyer. **Now all these things happened unto them for ensamples: and they are written for our admonition**, upon whom the ends of the world are come. Wherefore let him that thinketh he standeth take heed lest he fall.*

Why does God take time to tell us about those who were overthrown and destroyed in the Wilderness of Sin as He was leading Israel out of Egypt? The Lord holds these up for us as examples for our admonition so that we might take heed and not have our faith shipwrecked.

> *1 Timothy 1:18-19*
> *This charge I commit unto thee, son Timothy, according to the prophecies which went before on thee, **that thou by them mightest war a good warfare**; Holding faith, and a good conscience; which some having put away concerning faith have made shipwreck.*

To this, many will say, "It doesn't take all of that." Yet, only the uncircumcised try to drag the mess from the world into salvation while telling themselves it is okay. I am telling you that it takes all of this and more! Even after being sealed as one of God's people, your circumcision can become as uncircumcision (Romans 2:25). You can be engrafted into the vine, but later be cut off (John 15:6). You can start out on an exodus from Egypt, but be lost in the Wilderness of Sin trying to hold on to the things of Egypt (Numbers 14:28-35).

There are even people from whom you will have to depart simply because they are not going where you are going. You need to have a determined mind to make it in and your eye must be fixed on Jesus Christ so as not to be deterred. You have to recognize that you have been called to be a soldier. This is why God describes bringing Israel out of Egypt by their armies (Exodus 12:51). God knew the battles they would face in leaving Egypt and He was teaching their hands to war (Exodus 13:17).

What is God raising up now? An army. Most Christians do not perceive the need to be circumcised because they do not understand that we are in a spiritual war against the enemy of our souls. Having no idea what they have signed up for, most folks see church as a happy-go-lucky community meeting center for fellowship and to have a good time. However, there is no such thing in the New Testament.

Do you recall when Jesus encountered money changers in the temple? He said, "*You have made my Father's house a den of thieves and robbers. But my Father's house shall be called a house of prayer.*" (Isaiah 56:7; Matthew 21:13; Luke 19:46). The meaning of this verse is two-fold. Each believer is the temple of God and should be an individual house of prayer, praying without ceasing (1 Thessalonians 5:17). Further, the meeting place where you fellowship with other saints should be a house of prayer. In that place you might find teaching, edification, exhortation, prophecies, tongues, interpretation of tongues, etc. The church is wherever two or three are gathered together in Jesus' name (Matthew 18:20). Yet what do religious people do? They begin to worship that building over there sitting on ten acres of land saying, "Don't touch the communion table! It is consecrated unto the Lord." Many have been so brainwashed by religion that they don't understand that **we** are to be the vessels through whom Christ manifests. The believer is the only hope the world has. You don't go to Church to get right with God, you become the Church; and in order to do that you must go on an exodus. You have to move into another realm of living.

This is what God was preparing the Israelites to do. He reminds them of the covenant made with Abraham whereby every male child would be circumcised on the eighth day (Genesis 17:12). What does the number eight signify? Resurrection life. You circumcise yourself by cutting off the world through death to the old man on the cross, and God raises you as a spiritual man being dedicated to Him. I am leaving my fleshly, worldly life behind and entering into a covenant of faith in the living God. This is what God is after; an exodus leading to resurrected life as we become manifested sons of God.

A Vine Out of Egypt

Psalm 80:8-9
Thou hast brought a vine out of Egypt: thou hast cast out the heathen, and planted it. Thou preparedst room before it, and didst cause it to take deep root, and it filled the land.

God separated off a people unto Himself via the Abrahamic covenant by circumcising them from the world. They became an identifiable and peculiar people through the worship of the True and Living God. Although the Jews today in the nation of Israel must still be born again, they have at least identified the right God. They didn't receive the Messiah sent to save them, but they still worship the God of Abraham, Isaac, and Jacob. This is why all of the surrounding tribes hate Israel, both then and now. They resent the fact that Israel was chosen and they were not (Genesis 15:2-4; Deuteronomy 7:6).

This is also the inheritance of the church. The church did not replace Israel as some would say, but the church grew out of the loins of Israel (Romans 11:16-27). The initial believers were Jews, and the Gentiles have been engrafted into the faith because of them. God set apart the nation of Israel, not simply to make them a chosen people, but to accomplish a particular end: to have a people through whom He could reach the whole world. That is why I do not say anything detrimental against the Jewish people; those who do bring a curse upon themselves (Genesis 12:3, 27:29). Even the foolish prophet Balaam knew that he could not curse those whom God has blessed (Numbers 22:12). If you do not like the Jewish people, then you will never receive Jesus because He is a Jew; He came from the tribe of Judah.

Moses led the Israelites out of Egypt and into the wilderness as they headed towards the Promised Land. It is estimated that they totaled between two and three million people. In the wilderness, God calls Moses up to Mt. Sinai where He dictates to Moses the laws under which they must abide. God gives Israel commandments to sanctify and separate them. As Moses relayed God's commandments to Israel, God attested to the truthfulness of his words with a visual display of power. Thunder, lightning, smoke, and the sound of a trumpet appeared on the mountain, and the rest of Israel began to back away.

A manifestation of God snaps people back into reality as they are faced with the knowledge of with whom they are dealing. Even the Gospel is the power of God unto salvation (Romans 1:16). Just preach the true Gospel, you will see people begin to draw back away from you. The real Gospel message is unbearable to those who are not yet through with the world. This is why Israel said to Moses, *"Speak thou with us and we will hear, but let not God speak with us lest we die."* (Exodus 20:19-20). If that's not the modern day Christian, then I don't know what is. Yet Moses responded, *"Fear not for God has come to prove you."* Likewise, God also comes to prove us.

When faced with God's power, you come to understand that He is not someone to play with; He has the power to save or destroy you. This realization will either cause people to back up or draw nearer, based upon what is in the heart. The only thing that will keep you back from God is your love for sin. The Bible says that men love darkness rather than light because their deeds are evil. You will not draw close to the light if you still desire evil in your heart. Instead, you will step away because the truths of God irritate you and drive you off (2 Corinthians 2:15-16). The Gospel does not just save people, it will save or damn you based upon your response to it. The Gospel is specifically designed to either draw or drive you based upon what is inside of you.

The most common barrier that people put up between God and themselves is religion. They think, "The preacher, pastor, first lady, deacons, etc., they represent God. I'm just a lowly member of the congregation giving my tithe every week so that God won't get close to me." Since people do not want to be responsible or accountable to God, they set up a "Moses" to speak to them on God's behalf so as to not hear from God directly. They would rather worship a preacher over them instead of entering into communion with God to be changed.

Don't forget, time spent in communion with God will change you into His image as you begin to radiate His glory. However, if you are not personally accountable and responsible before God, then you will not be transformed. Instead, you will wind up in Hell because only those remade into the image of Christ make it in (Romans 8:29-30). The Bible says seek the Lord while He is near for the day comes when no one will find Him (Isaiah 55:6; Jeremiah 29:12-14). Work while it's day because the time is coming when no man can work (John 9:4). You have to draw near to God and seek to see Him face to face. Jesus has made a way for *every human* to come before the living God, even unto the Holiest of Holies.

When Jesus and the disciples preached the Gospel, many departed from them. Yet they made no move to go after those who departed. It is what it is. You decide your eternal destiny - whether you go to Heaven or to Hell - by your response to the proclaimed word of God. Each individual must make up his or her mind now for time is short. Whosoever will, come drink of the waters which are freely given (Revelation 22:17).

An angel goes before the Israelites to lead them into the Promised Land and deliver them from the surrounding demonic tribes. He commanded Israel to break down the images of the foreign tribes and their gods so as not to go into idolatry. In the New Testament these images are our own imaginations. Just as Israel was to break down these idolatrous images, we are to cast down demonic imaginations which have infiltrated the soul. Every high thing which exalts itself against the knowledge of Christ must be brought into the obedience of Christ (2 Corinthians 10:5). The idolatrous images in your mind coming from these foreign entities will prevent you from advancing into the kingdom of God. Satan loves to mock the ignorance of church folks as he presents various shows and movies depicting man battling against supernatural, demonic giants - which the world often refers to as aliens. Yet we know from Scripture that these are the nephilim; the giants produced when the fallen angels produced offspring with the daughters of men (Genesis 6:1-4). These images from Satan are designed to make your enemies seem invincible and larger than life so that you will appear as mere "*grasshoppers*" in your own eyes (Numbers 13:33). Unless these images are cast down, you will never confront the enemy. We need to repent and go on an exodus.

Exodus 23:25-30
And ye shall serve the LORD your God, and he shall bless
thy bread, and thy water; and I will take sickness away from

the midst of thee. There shall nothing cast their young, nor be barren, no barren wombs, no premature births, in thy land: the number of thy days I will fulfil. I will send my fear before thee, and will destroy all the people to whom thou shalt come, and I will make all thine enemies turn their backs unto thee. And I will send hornets before thee, which shall drive out the Hivite, the Canaanite, and the Hittite, from before thee. I will not drive them out from before thee in one year; lest the land become desolate, and the beast of the field multiply against thee. **By little and little I will drive them out from before thee, until thou be increased, and inherit the land.**

Look at the blessings for those who obey God in this exodus to the Promised Land. You will fulfill all the days God has appointed for you; nobody's life will be cut short. He will send the Devil on the run, which is the way it should be. The reason the Devil has been down here raining havoc on people's lives is because the church has not gone on an exodus to purge the inner man. Since the Devil still has access to the church through the lusts of the flesh, God's power in our lives is short-circuited.

To address this, God is going to drive out these demonic tribes in your soul "*little by little*" until you can possess the whole land. In your patience, you will possess your soul. He will not get rid of them all at one time because we would not be able to handle it. He says to do that would make our land desolate and the beasts would multiply against us.

Matthew 12:43-45
When the unclean spirit is gone out of a man, he walketh through dry places, seeking rest, and findeth none. Then he saith, I will return into my house from whence I came out; and when he is come, **he findeth it empty, swept, and garnished. Then goeth he, and taketh with himself seven other spirits more wicked than himself, and they enter in and dwell there: and the last state of that man is worse than the first.** *Even so shall it be also unto this wicked generation.*

God is calling us to possess the land and occupy it. Yet, if He drives off every foreign thing at once, we would not be strong enough to safeguard that which He has committed to us (2 Timothy 1:14). The Devil is not *replaced*, he is *displaced*. As you feed on the word of God, stay in prayer and fasting, and sanctify yourself unto the Lord, the Holy Ghost continues to fill you. You will see God's presence increase within as you get power to drive the devil off and take over the territory he inhabited, i.e., your emotions, feelings, perceptions, inclinations, idiosyncrasies, and thoughts. **All** of these areas are spiritual parameters which the devil has been accessing most of your life.

This is why God says that we must be renewed in the spirit of our minds (Ephesians 4:23). Our minds and very way of thinking have been contaminated through years of interaction with the devil and his perverse world. So the Spirit of God must come to restore, renovate, regenerate, and reconcile. He has to make us over from the inside out. However, He cannot do this if we are continuing to ingest food from the filthy world. A double minded man is unstable in **all** of his ways and should not think that he will receive anything from the Lord (James 1:6-8).

The land increases against you because you keep going back to the same sin from which God has delivered you. Yet this time, it is coming back with reinforcements to make it harder for you to get free. You stop fornicating and come to Jesus, but then you go back to fornication. You had better know that all kinds of perverse spirits came back this time. Now you are not only a fornicator, but you are into all types of illicit sexual activity as you are driven by a lust you cannot control. The addiction will not only be deeper and more perverse, it will be a bigger stronghold than it was before. The human body was not designed by God to be a dwelling place of demons and you will literally drive yourself insane fooling around with unclean spirits. You can experience the powerful deliverance of God and choose to go back to the vomit if you want to, but you will become an animal, a beast (2 Peter 2:22).

This is why people back away from the real Gospel; they are not yet through with sin. You are either in covenant with demons or in covenant with God. If you have not made up your mind to turn away from the world and turn towards the Lord with your whole heart, then you are damning yourselves to Hell by playing games with God. Look at what He tells Israel as they prepare to possess the land.

Exodus 23:31-33
*And I will set thy bounds from the Red sea even unto the sea of the Philistines, and from the desert unto the river: for **I will deliver the inhabitants of the land into your hands; and thou shalt drive them out** before thee. **Thou shalt make no covenant with them, nor with their gods.** They shall not dwell in thy land, **lest they make thee sin against me**: for if thou serve their gods, it will surely be a snare unto thee.*

God has wrought deliverance on behalf on His people. He has ensured that we have the power to overcome the giants, but **we** must drive them out. Yet, we cannot drive them out if we are in covenant with them. Covenant is an agreement; we can have no covenant or agreement with the Devil.

If the Devil says left, I say right. If the Devil says down, I'll say up. There can be no agreement with Satan. When the Bible speaks to Israel about the gods of these foreign tribes, for us it means the fallen angels and the demons. We are to make no covenant with them or with their unclean spirits or else they will cause us to sin. If you serve the fallen angels and the demons they sired, it will ensnare and bind you. The New Testament puts it this way:

2 Corinthians 6:15-18
*And **what concord hath Christ with Belial**? Or what part hath he that believeth with an infidel? And what agreement hath the temple of God with idols? For ye are the temple of the living God; as God hath said, I will dwell in them, and walk in them; and I will be their God, and they shall be my people. Wherefore come out from among them, and be ye separate, saith the Lord, and touch not the unclean thing; and I will receive you, And will be a Father unto you, and ye shall be my sons and daughters, saith the Lord Almighty.*

You cannot have any agreement with demons because God is preparing us as His temples, His dwelling place. God is light and He desires to illuminate and light us up as lights unto the world. He is making us His sons and daughters.

As Israel keeps moving into the Promised Land, they only need to obey Him to ensure the success He has promised. However, not ten chapters later they are worshipping at a golden calf. As soon as Moses was not around, they fell into idolatry.

Exodus 32:21-26
And Moses said unto Aaron, What did this people unto thee, that thou hast brought so great a sin upon them? And Aaron said, Let not the anger of my lord wax hot: thou knowest the people, that they are set on mischief. For they said unto me, Make us gods, which shall go before us: for as for this Moses, the man that brought us up out of the land of Egypt, we wot not what is become of him. And I said unto them, Whosoever hath any gold, let them break it off. So they gave

*it me: then I cast it into the fire, and there came out this
calf. And when Moses saw that the people were naked; (for
Aaron had made them naked unto their shame among their
enemies:) Then Moses stood in the gate of the camp, and
said, Who is on the LORD'S side? Let him come unto me.
And all the sons of Levi gathered themselves together unto
him. And he said unto them, Thus saith the LORD God of
Israel, Put every man his sword by his side, and go in and
out from gate to gate throughout the camp, and slay every
man his brother, and every man his companion, and every
man his neighbour. And the children of Levi did according
to the word of Moses: and there fell of the people that day
about three thousand men.*

Without Moses in sight, the people eagerly and readily fall into sin.
Where does all of this come from? Egypt. They had seen this idolatry in
Egypt and it contaminated them. What is the golden calf to us? Anything
we exalt over the word of God. Today, the world lets anyone be an authority
on how we are supposed to live. Someone can be divorced, shacking up,
homosexual or living in any kind of rebellion to God, and people will pay
heed to them before they will obey the Lord. A lot of people don't like what
I'm saying right now because they identify more with the golden calf than
they do with the living God!

Yet what does Aaron do when confronted by Moses? He quickly
minimizes his role in the idolatry and blames the people. He might as well
have said, *"The people made me do it. They didn't know where you were
and gave me gold to make an idol. I cast the gold into the fire and, 'Poof',
out came this calf."* Now you know someone had to mold the gold into the
calf. That is fallen man for you; he can never be responsible or accountable
before God. It is always someone else's fault, just as with Adam in the Garden
of Eden when he said, *"The woman whom thou gavest to be with me, she
gave me of the tree, and I did eat."* (Genesis 3:12)

Yet God is not mocked. He always goes straight to the one in authority
to demand an account of what has happened. The Scripture says, *"for **Aaron**
had made them naked unto their shame among their enemies."* God didn't
fall for excuses then and He won't now. Aaron was the one left in charge, so
he was accountable.

Paul the Apostle said, *"When I depart there is no man like me who
would care for you or be concerned about your spiritual wherewithal at all
because each man seeks after his own."* (Philippians 2:20-21). That is how
people are even today. This is why this exodus has to be personal to you. You
have to want to make it for yourself, and not anyone else. Anyone can die.

Anyone can fall by the wayside. You cannot make it depending upon anyone else; it must be your own **personal** conviction.

The only representation Israel received of God was Moses; and when the cat is away, the mice will play. Most Christians have no significant awareness of God personally because they are hiding behind a Moses. They put on a show in the church environment, but outside of that they revert right back to type: stinking filthy sinners, fornicating, drinking liquor, watching pornography, cutting the fool and living like hell. People claim to be saved, but live and look just like the world. Such are Egyptians, and you had better go on an exodus **away** from them. It is not about what I say or agreeing with me; look at the Scriptures for yourselves! This is not about being legalistic, but running this race towards your own freedom and not letting anything or anyone get in your way. It is about what the Lord says and the separation that is necessary to serve the Lord in spirit and in truth.

Understand that the people were naked physically and spiritually while worshipping the golden calf. The protection of God had lifted from them due to their sin and they were in a naked orgy like animals. So what does God do? He separates them. He draws a line between those who will serve the Lord and those who will not and kills off those who are against Him. He purged the camp. What is God doing now in the church? He's purging the church. He's making it so hot, that the sinner will not be able to stand in it. The Bible says that if the righteous scarcely be saved, where will the sinner and the ungodly appear (1 Peter 4:18)?

Either you will turn back yourself or God will stop you Himself, but you cannot go on this exodus with the filth of the world embedded in your soul. If you have been in the truth any length of time, you have seen the number of people who have turned away from it. You want to be among the number who make it in.

The Fruit of Love

The laws given to Israel were directly related to what they were encountering on the exodus. God gave them laws to counteract what the sinners were doing around them as well as to address what was within their own hearts through slavery to Egypt. No matter what, the law was not downgraded for anyone, and neither will God change His standard of righteousness for us. The law says do not tattoo your body, yet people have a cross tattooed on their arm. Why do they do this? Because they want to look like, and identify with, the world. They are an Egyptian, attempting to Christianize the demonic rituals of the world. If you received tattoos before you got saved, repent. Ask God to forgive you of what was done in ignorance.

The law says it is an abomination to lie with a man as you would with a woman. So what do you do if you have participated in homosexuality? Repent. The only thing keeping you alive is the grace, mercy, and longsuffering of Jesus Christ as He gives you time. Repent and turn away from what you are doing. Staying in covenant with it will damn your soul. Anyone who tells you different is a liar and the truth is not in them. You cannot stay in sin and make it in; it doesn't work that way. You have to keep moving from glory to glory (2 Corinthians 3:18). We are on an exodus away from the world and into the promises of God. Every law, rule, and regulation was to keep Israel separated from the tribes around them so that they would not become defiled.

What was God looking for? Their obedience. The battle had been already won; God had already given them the land. All they needed to do was **believe** Him and go in to possess it. You see, belief is not just a mental position; true belief is accompanied by action (James 2:18-26). Today you have millions of people who identify themselves as Christians, yet they are not true believers because they do not obey the Lord. They are like the Israelites in the Wilderness of Sin.

> *Numbers 13:30-33*
> *And Caleb stilled the people before Moses, and said, Let us go up at once, and possess it; for **we are well able to overcome it**. But the men that went up with him said, We be not able to go up against the people; for they are stronger than we. And they brought up an evil report of the land which they had searched unto the children of Israel, saying, The land, through which we have gone to search it, is a land that eateth up the inhabitants thereof; and all the people that we saw in it are men of a great stature. And there we saw the giants, the sons of Anak, which come of the giants: and we were in our own sight as grasshoppers, and so we were in their sight.*

The evidence that Israel did not believe God is seen in that they did not **obey** him. God had commanded them to go in and possess the land, yet they insisted that they could not. Instead of trusting in God and esteeming His riches more than that of the Egyptians, the people murmured and complained against God, protesting that His way was too hard. Because they still yearned for Egypt in their hearts, they saw themselves as defeated and small. What were they afraid to face? The giants, the nephilim, the demons. Being still in covenant with Egypt in their hearts, they could not - and would not - come against the demonic tribes in the land.

Numbers 14:2-4, 21-24
And all the children of Israel murmured against Moses and against Aaron: and the whole congregation said unto them, Would God that we had died in the land of Egypt! Or would God we had died in this wilderness! And wherefore hath the LORD brought us unto this land, to fall by the sword, that our wives and our children should be a prey? **Were it not better for us to return into Egypt?** *And they said one to another, Let us make a captain, and let us return into Egypt...*
But as truly as I live, all the earth shall be filled with the glory of the LORD. Because all those men which have seen my glory, and my miracles, which I did in Egypt and in the wilderness, **and have tempted me now these ten times,** *and have not hearkened to my voice; Surely they shall not see the land which I sware unto their fathers, neither shall any of them that provoked me see it:* **But my servant Caleb, because he had another spirit with him, and hath followed me fully, him will I bring into the land** *whereinto he went; and his seed shall possess it.*

Except for Caleb and Joshua, the Israelites were still carnal. They did not have a spiritual mind to perceive and walk in the things of God. Remember, the carnal mind is the enemy of God and is therefore not subject to the law of God. No matter how much one claims to belong to God, continued disobedience to Him is the sign that you are still carnal and He will not receive you as His own. Because of Israel's continued disobedience, God stated that He would disinherit them (Numbers 14:12). They would not be partakers of the Promised Land.

God is longsuffering, working mercifully with us to turn our hearts completely towards Him. God did not disinherit the people He delivered from Egypt at their first transgression. Rather, He continued to demonstrate His love, grace, and power to them throughout their time in the Wilderness of Sin; yet still they would not change. As Jesus said, many times He longed to take them unto Himself, but they would not (Matthew 23:37; Luke 13:34).

God had to cleanse Israel from the defilements of Egypt by sending them into the Wilderness of Sin for forty years before they could enter into His promises. Those who refused to be purged from Egypt died in that same wilderness, still bound by sin. Now look at the numbers. Although millions were originally delivered from Egypt, the only ones of that original number to make it into the Promised Land were Joshua and Caleb. Everyone else born in Egypt refused to let go of it and remained tied to it in their souls, so God let them die. Two out of millions, made it in, yet people still want to claim that salvation is not that serious and it doesn't take all this. Many are called, but the chosen are few (Matthew 22:14).

Remember, we are going on an exodus and you cannot take the things from Egypt with you into the Promised Land. Anything contrary to God will need to be left behind. We will continue to wander in the Wilderness of Sin - never entering the Promised Land - until we obey Him.

Obedience is not a work; it is the fruit of love. Jesus said that if we love God, then we will obey His commands (John 14:15, 15:10; 1 John 5:2-3). Just as with Israel, every command that God gives in the New Testament is to keep you free from the demons. You have been delivered from Egypt and are now going through the wilderness in order to learn to obey (love) Him. Only then will you be able to confront your enemies and receive your inheritance. Like Caleb & Joshua, we must be overcomers, and for that to occur we must obey God.

Immediately after Israel enters the Promised Land, the Bible transitions to the book of Judges. The Lord set up judges over His people to keep them under His yoke and obedient to His commands. God is setting apart a people so that He can establish among them a tabernacle unto Himself.

The Bible is not written haphazardly. It outlines the **movement of a people** from Genesis through the Abrahamic covenant down into Egypt and into a land where the Lord can bring about the manifestation of Jesus Christ. That is why it was so important for God to sanctify His people. He had to set apart a people who were worshippers of the True and Living God so that the Messiah of the world, Jesus Christ, would not be born to idolaters. The coming of Jesus Christ was not simply to benefit Israel; it was to be a blessing to all the nations of the earth. This is why the book of Judges is followed by the book of Ruth. Even those who were not naturally born as an Israelite can benefit from God's blessings. How? By going on an exodus and leaving behind all which is of the world; even all their possessions and people they have known. Whether Jew or Gentile, everyone who would be reconciled to God must go on an exodus, forsaking that which is familiar so as to follow Him. Everything in the Bible is logical, but you must have spiritual eyes to see it.

In His love, God was preparing a people through whom the Savior would come to bless all the nations of the earth.

The Harvest is Ripe

Joel 3:9-14
Proclaim ye this among the Gentiles; Prepare war, wake
up the mighty men, let all the men of war draw near; let
them come up: Beat your plowshares into swords and your
pruninghooks into spears: let the weak say, I am strong.
Assemble yourselves, and come, all ye heathen, and gather
yourselves together round about: thither cause thy mighty
ones to come down, O Lord. Let the heathen be wakened,
and come up to the valley of Jehoshaphat: for there will
I sit to judge all the heathen round about. Put ye in the
sickle, for the harvest is ripe: come, get you down; for the
press is full, the fats overflow; for their wickedness is great.
Multitudes, multitudes in the valley of decision: for the day
of the Lord is near in the valley of decision.

God had led the people out of Egypt, purged them in the Wilderness of Sin, given them commands to keep them from being defiled by the demonic tribes, and taken them into the Promised Land. He had shown Himself strong in delivering them from their enslavement and giving them victory over their enemies. Yet, what did the people do? They chose to set up a King over themselves. They still wanted to be like the surrounding tribes. They wanted a King they could visibly see and in whom they could glory. As with Moses, the people still wanted someone to intercede for them on God's behalf so that they would not have to deal with Him directly. They did not want to be directly accountable or responsible before God.

Today, that King is called "Pastor". People want to have some kind of charismatic personality over them whom they can boast in and hide behind as a validation that they belong to God. Yet, there are no personality cults in this. You must get individually full of the Holy Ghost and personally represent Christ in the earth yourself to be accounted worthy to enter in amongst the entourage of the saints in heaven.

Did not Jesus say that salvation is rare (Matthew 7:14)? It is a radical transformation which requires your complete commitment to it. It is not God's will to have an intermediary between you and Him; God took the people's desire for such as a personal rejection of His lordship over them (1 Samuel 8:7-8). Why do people run to a King or a Pastor instead of serving God directly? They don't want to obey God; they don't want God telling them what to do. Therefore they choose instead to be pleasers of men; such persons will never be acceptable to God (Galatians 1:10). God even tells them what will happen if they choose to serve men over Himself.

> *1 Samuel 8:11-20*
> *And he said, This will be the manner of the king that shall reign over you: He will take your sons, and appoint them for himself, for his chariots, and to be his horsemen; and some shall run before his chariots. And he will appoint him captains over thousands, and captains over fifties; and will set them to ear his ground, and to reap his harvest, and to make his instruments of war, and instruments of his chariots. And he will take your daughters to be confectionaries, and to be cooks, and to be bakers. And he will take your fields, and your vineyards, and your oliveyards, even the best of them, and give them to his servants. And he will take the tenth of your seed, and of your vineyards, and give to his officers, and to his servants. And he will take your menservants, and your maidservants, and your goodliest young men, and your asses, and put them to his work. He will take the tenth of your sheep: and ye shall be his servants. And ye shall cry out in that day because of your king which ye shall have chosen you; and the LORD will not hear you in that day. Nevertheless the people refused to obey the voice of Samuel; and they said, Nay; but we will have a king over us; That we also may be like all the nations; and that our king may judge us, and go out before us, and fight our battles.*

This is exactly what self-professed lords over God's inheritance will do (1 Peter 5:2-3). They will enslave you and your children in servitude to themselves while taking all of your possessions for their own use. They will take 10% of your earnings and falsely call it a tithe commanded by God. Yet still the people desired a Saul over them, and God let them have exactly what they wanted. As a result, Saul did unto the people all that God had forewarned.

Saul's real sin is that he only half-heartedly obeyed God, and to obey half of what God says is to still be in disobedience. Because he was not led by the Spirit of God, Saul had to turn to witchcraft and sorcery in order to maintain a show of godliness (2 Timothy 3:1-8).

This half-hearted obedience is evidenced in many Christians today. They have no real zeal or drive to serve the Lord. They just hang around saved folk and hope to make it in by association. This is why false churches draw thousands of followers; the people are hiding out in the crowds. Yet God has called each of us to be a soldier and we need to be personally engaged in this war. If you need a volunteer to go to the front lines, I want to be the first one in. I'll carry the banner. I'm leading the charge, no matter who is or is not coming. I have my sword drawn and I am ready to fight this good fight of faith. This is how you must be. Why should I be dragging in behind, not knowing if I'm going to make it; just hoping that I am saved? We each need to make our calling and election sure.

God's answer to Saul was to raise up David, a man after His own heart. God had to anoint someone who would not abuse His people, but would be a warrior to help sanctify the people from their enemies. Once the people were sanctified, God would have a tabernacle where He could dwell amongst His people. While it took war to secure a place for the temple, the temple itself would be established in peace. This is why Solomon was chosen after King David to establish the temple (1 Chronicles 22:2-10, 23:3).

Remember, the Old Testament is a shadow of God's ultimate plans revealed in the New Testament. God's exodus and sanctification of the people are necessary in order for Him to erect a temple wherein He can dwell. These Old Testament figures are an illustration of what He is doing in us. God is building Himself a home in us because our bodies are to be the temple of the living God (1 Corinthians 6:19). It will take a spiritual war to possess our souls, overcoming the enemies who try to lead us into sin. Only then, once we have overcome the enemy, can we experience the peace of God within.

The construction of the temple itself mirrors the exodus we take into the spiritual realm where God abides. The temple had three major components: an outer court, inner court, and the Holy of Holies. When we organically grow from being time and space centered to be Heavenly focused, we go on a spiritual exodus from being in the outer court (fleshly), through the inner court (soulish), into God's presence in the Holy of Holies (spiritual). This exodus depends upon self-denial as with each step closer to God you are leaving something else behind.

In the outer court, you have the brazen laver full of water where the priests washed themselves. This symbolizes you being cleansed as the defilements from the world are washed off of you. From there, the priests would progress into the inner court where the candlestick and shewbread were housed. This represents your having a renewed mind as you receive the engrafted word of God which has been illuminated to you by the Holy Spirit. Entering into the Holy of Holies, the priests would pass through a billowing altar of incense from the golden censors as they came before the ark of the covenant. The ark contained the law of God, a pot of manna, and Aaron's rod which had budded. Now having a pure heart of belief, we are able to lift up praise, worship, and spiritual prayers as represented by the incense. Being in God's presence, we walk in obedience to Him (the law) through partaking of the bread of life (Jesus) and are granted priestly authority (Aaron's rod budded).

It all depicts an exodus. It is a journey into obedience to God as you become one with Him through fellowship with the Son, with evidential authority of God testifying to who you are in Christ. That is when you know that you are a child of God.

In the New Testament you leave the realm of the flesh (the outer court) and travel through your soul to get into the spirit. When you were a sinner, you lived in the flesh. Your appetites were worldly and the things of the world drew upon the lusts of your flesh. If the things of the world still appeal to you, then guess what? You need to be born again. You need to be saved for real, because the things of the flesh hold no appeal to those who are born after the spirit. Once you are born again, you will come out from amongst them and touch not the unclean thing as God receives you unto Himself.

After salvation, you go through the process of transformation of the soul in the inner court. Your soul has to be reconditioned, reformatted, and restored to actually walk in the spirit. Why? Because just as God told Israel on their exodus, this way is foreign to you; you have never been this way before. In order to walk in the spirit, your soul has to be taught to be led by the spirit and not the flesh. All of your life, you have done what was right in your own eyes as your soul has taken dictates from your flesh - what you think, feel, taste, touch, hear, etc. Now your soul must learn to instead submit to your spirit, which is receiving input from the Spirit of God. We cannot go it on our own because we do not know the way. Rather, by day and by night, we must follow the Lord (Exodus 13:21-22).

Having been washed and sanctified, we are ready to reach our destination: God's presence. This requires us to be in the spirit, for that is where He is. We must worship God in what? In spirit and in truth. You must have your soul reformatted by the Spirit of God to understand truth before you can offer the worship He desires. Jesus' flesh was rent so that His healing blood would flow, cleansing us from all that was done through our association with the world. Similarly, the veil separating us from God's presence was also rent so that we can now boldly approach the throne of grace (Hebrews 10:19-23).

Romans 3:21-27
But now the righteousness of God without the law is
manifested before, being witnessed by the law and the

prophets; Even the righteousness of God which is by faith of Jesus Christ unto all and upon all them that believe: for there is no difference: For all have sinned, and come short of the glory of God; Being justified freely by his grace through the redemption that is in Christ Jesus: through faith in his blood, to declare his righteousness for the remission...or washing away of sins that are past, through the forbearance of God; to declare, I say, at this time his righteousness: that he might be just, and the justifier of him which believes in Jesus. Where is boasting then? It is excluded. By what law? Of works? Nay: but by the law of faith.

A propitiation is a mercy seat or an atoning victim. Jesus was an atoning victim and He alone qualifies you to receive what God has provided. God is patiently dealing with us to bring us to repentance. There is nothing from which we can boast for faith is the gift of God. You cannot believe unless God gives you the ability to believe. However, you cannot be given the ability to believe unless you repent and turn away from the world. The Gospel is presented for you to be confronted with truth. For those who submit to it and turn away from the lies you believed in the world, faith is given to begin this journey. If you do not turn away from the world, you will always be seeking a way to return to Egypt or to build an idolatrous golden calf to carry along with you. You will always gravitate to that which is familiar; something you can smell, taste, or touch because you are still living according to the flesh. You will seek some man or woman in whom to trust instead of God and thereby place yourself under a curse as your heart departs from the Lord (Jeremiah 17:5).

For those who receive this propitiation through repentance, we begin an exodus headed towards one result: entering into the promises of God.

Aaron's Rod Budding

Numbers 17:1-8
*And the LORD spake unto Moses, saying, Speak unto the children of Israel, and take of every one of them a rod according to the house of their fathers, of all their princes according to the house of their fathers twelve rods: write thou every man's name upon his rod. **And thou shalt write Aaron's name upon the rod of Levi**: for one rod shall be for the head of the house of their fathers. And thou shalt*

*lay them up in the tabernacle of the congregation before the testimony, where I will meet with you. **And it shall come to pass, that the man's rod, whom I shall choose, shall blossom**: and I will make to cease from me the murmurings of the children of Israel, whereby they murmur against you. And Moses spake unto the children of Israel, and every one of their princes gave him a rod apiece, for each prince one, according to their fathers' houses, even twelve rods: and the rod of Aaron was among their rods. And Moses laid up the rods before the LORD in the tabernacle of witness. And it came to pass, that on the morrow Moses went into the tabernacle of witness; **and, behold, the rod of Aaron for the house of Levi was budded, and brought forth buds, and bloomed blossoms, and yielded almonds.***

In ancient times, a rod was often a symbol of power, authority, and rulership. From this text we see that each tribe was commanded to present Moses with a rod to be placed in the temple. God was doing this to address the dissenters amongst the people who questioned God's authority. The impetus of the dispute was whether Israel should enter the Promised Land or whether they were better off returning to Egypt (Numbers 14:1-4). Korah, Dathan, and Abiram began to contest the leadership of Moses and Aaron and amassed a company of Israelites to rebel with them. They didn't just assemble any men, but they chose men of renown; those who were known and of reputation amongst the people (Numbers 16:2).

Before you go one step further, know that your decision to go into the Promised Land will be a separator between you and others who decide to go back to the world. The opposition will be **strong** and **fierce**. It will not just be every day Joes who stand against you, but some of the most popular Christian personalities will tell you that it doesn't take all of that. They will claim that you do not have to cross into the Promised Land; you can stay in the comforts of Egypt and still serve the Lord. Do not fall for their deceptions. They are enemies to your soul and enemies to the cross of Jesus. To stem this rebellion, God destroyed Korah, Dathan, Abiram, and all of their families as the earth opened up to swallow them alive (Numbers 16:29-35). Further, fire came out from the Lord and destroyed all who followed after them. God is serious about us possessing the land and He will consume anything that tries to block our way. These false prophets and lying wonders will be judged by the Lord.

Once the dissention had been addressed, God settled this matter once and for all by designating the one whom He chose as the head of the house of their fathers. Many were called to submit their rods in the temple, but only one was chosen; and that one was Aaron's rod.

This presentation of Aaron's rod budding is an illustration of what God is after in all of us. Aaron's rod was designated as representing the tribe of Levi, who comprised the Levitical priesthood of the Old Testament. In the New Testament, believers in Christ are the royal priesthood chosen in Christ (1 Peter 2:9).

When God manifests the ones He has chosen, there is no need for further discussion. People can debate and go back and forth all day, but when the sons of God become manifested, there are no more questions. Either we have the life of God in us or we don't. Either God's power is flowing through us and His fruit visible within us or it is not.

Aaron's rod budded, blossomed, and bore fruit. Typically, there is an order and progression to organic growth (Matthew 4:28). A tree buds, then the buds turn into blossoms, and finally the blossoms bear fruit. Yet, all stages of growth were reflected in this rod at one time. In this miraculous display, God manifests the entire organic growth cycle in one moment as an illustration of what He is after in man. Similarly, only those who have gone through this process of organic growth to bear fruit in Christ will be chosen by God in the end. They will be fruitful because they have abided in the vine.

The word Levi itself means "joined to or attached". Only those who remain attached to Jesus can bear fruit. Each rod started off as a branch of wood broken off from its source of life. Initially, they all appeared outwardly as dead sticks; you could not tell the difference between them. The separator was the manifestation of life. As with the wheat and the tares, at the time of harvest, the difference in fruitfulness between them becomes apparent (Matthew 13:24-30). This is the distinction between those who believe Jesus from the heart and have gone through the organic processes of being transformed into Christ versus those who have never sanctified themselves from the world. One will bear forth manifestation of the life of Christ within and one will not.

It is the rod of Aaron which God used to swallow up the Egyptian magicians' serpents. God displayed His power through Aaron's rod in bringing about many of the plagues of judgment against Egypt. Aaron's rod was the one used to part the Red Sea in delivering Israel out of Egypt. We need the authority of the priesthood which comes from the manifested life of God within to confound the sorceries of Babylon and set souls free. If we have anything short of God-ordained spiritual authority and the resurrected life of Christ within, then we will fail in our attempt to minister to others. How do we walk in the power, authority, and rulership of Christ in these last days? We must be turned from dead sticks into living branches having budded, blossomed, and borne fruit by abiding in Christ. This requires an exodus.

You cannot hang around the same people from the world and think you are going on an exodus. Evil communications corrupt good manners (1 Corinthians 15:33). You may have to leave some people alone because they are not going where you are going. You must be willing to walk out your faith alone, for any one individual could decide that they are going no further and stop along the way. Husbands, wives, sisters, brothers, butchers, bakers, candlestick makers...**everybody** must be placed on the altar so that you can make it in (Luke 14:26).

Salvation is all about organic growth from being that which was by nature carnal to becoming that which is by nature spiritual. This growth will take you on a vertical exodus from being time and space-centered to being Heavenly focused. As Israel had to *go* into the Promised Land, we must *grow* into the Promised Land as Christ is formed within us. I am going on an exodus to be molded into the image of Jesus Christ, and whatever hinders me in this journey must be overcome.

Each person must have their own individual relationship with God and their own lineage of spiritual people whom they have helped to bring into the Kingdom. Where is that which has come out of your own loins because you are able to reproduce after your own kind? It is terrifying to consider that most church folks have no evidence of spiritual life in them. They cannot reproduce the life they claim to possess because the truth is that they have yet to possess it. They just sit around in theater style seating yelling, "Amen!" to something somebody says. That is garbage and has nothing to do with New Testament life or the Gospel.

God's goal is glorification. He is leading you out of Egypt in order to glorify you so that He can use you and move through you. You go from Egypt, you head through the Wilderness of Sin and the destination is the Promised Land. You will encounter barriers on the way, but God gave dictates all through the Old Testament to keep them on course.

Throughout the Bible, God uses different analogies, but He is referring to the same process each time. These stages illustrate the organic growth we all must go through in salvation.

Seed of life -> Germination -> Fruitfulness
Egypt -> Wilderness of Sin -> Promised Land
Outer Court -> Inner Court -> Holy of Holies
Alive to the world -> Crucified with Christ -> Resurrected Life
Flesh -> Soul -> Spirit
World conscious -> Self Conscious -> God Conscious

The natural state of fallen man is to be conscious of the world. When you are world-conscious, all you are concerned about is how you look to the world. This perspective makes you want to be accepted and esteemed by the world. Your focus then is on what kind of car you drive, where you live, how much money you have, etc. You use the things of the world to try and look like something.

When you get saved, you will naturally start to back out of the world, but you then become self-conscious. People spend all of their time in church, examining themselves. They say, *"The Lord did this for me...the Lord told me...I was thinking the other day about my life and where I come from..."* It is a constant stream of me, myself, and I. No one wants to hear that.

Do you have a witness for Christ? Do you have anything to say about salvation? Do you have any exhortation, edification or comfort for the saints? No one is that interested in you! I preach the gospel all of the time, but I am not the focus of the message. I am pointing you to Christ. Church is not a place for you to see a psychologist. You examine yourself to see if you are in the faith, but you should not stay there.

The goal is to become God conscious. Your mind is focused on knowing and obeying the commands of God. I care about what God cares about. I see my life through the eyes of God. I'm not conscious of the world, nor do I care what they think about me. We don't need recognition by anyone except God. He knows what you do in the quietness of your prayer closet for other people's souls. I don't care what I think about myself because I know my righteousness is just filthy rags. My affections are set upon the Holy One of Israel. Your mind has to be radically transformed and renewed to become God conscious. All of us who are conscious of God can walk in a like, precious faith because we only care about what God thinks. We are not here to talk about me and you all day. It gets stale and old when somebody sits and talks about themselves all the time.

On this exodus, you are not looking for anyone to validate you because you are accepted in the Beloved. You do not need people to "Amen!" what you say or give you accolades. I'm looking for the Lord Jesus Christ and believing in Him unto righteousness and salvation. You won't need to be a part of anything or affiliated with anyone. Because of organic growth, you no longer have to pretend or change from place to place for being like Christ is not something you try to do, it is who you have become. Since you possess the life of Christ within, you will have your own lineage of people brought into the faith because each life produces after its own kind.

There is no joy for anyone to be lost. This is our responsibility as saints. This is an exodus away from the world into the deeper recesses of God. We're coming out of Egypt and into the presence of God. We are arriving at the Promised Land, at the Holy of Holies. We are arriving at a place inside of God's Spirit where we can walk in the consciousness of God on a daily basis in fruitfulness. This is the Promised Land where resurrected life has given us access to the Holy of Holies. In the Spirit, we are so focused on God that His thoughts become our thoughts and His ways become our ways as we give ourselves over to Him. This is our destination.

Where are the people that are being born again from you being a living witness? Where are the sign and gifts as promised in Mark 16:15-20? Where is the power of God that demonstrates that God is upon you and living in you? You can kid yourself all the way through this, yet no one believes it. People will sit right in a church pew week after week and convince themselves through mental ascension that they're saved.

According to God's word, the end times have begun and we have to be made conformable to the death of Christ in order to walk in resurrection life. There is no time for games; no time to fool around or kid ourselves. The entire world is awaiting the manifestation of the body of Christ **right now**. For the sake of millions, if not billions, of souls that are lost in a delusion, we need to be that body. We must pray for the intestinal fortitude to do whatever is necessary so that we might be conformed into the image of Jesus Christ. Only if we are like Him can we reflect Him to the world as He draws men unto Himself (John 12:32).

We cannot approach this with head knowledge void of a heart change. We must truly repent and truly believe. The more I repent, the more I acknowledge and come into agreement with what God has shown me about myself. He is continually showing you that which still has you tied to this world and needs to be crucified. He's showing you yourself along this Exodus as He reveals your own soul to you. Where are the enemies of your soul encamped? Where are the strongholds? God will reveal this to you by the Holy Ghost. The spirit of man is the candle of the Lord searching the innermost parts of the human (Proverbs 20:27). He's showing you yourself, for a reason: so that you may launch a successful war against the enemies of your soul and enter into His promises.

If you are crucified with Christ, then you will not be alive to the things of the world. I am not just speaking of lust for things; your own experiences and perceptions in life can bind you. Hatred, pride, rejection, hurts, and a desire to be liked by others are all things outside of the Spirit of God which can tie you to this present, evil world and make you controllable by the god of this world. When you respond to the Devil and his schemes, you are letting him dictate your life. Your very response to him gives him power over you in getting you to react to his inputs. You must get moving on an exodus with the mission of the Almighty God who saved you.

If you want to make it back to your Bridegroom and His Father, then you must follow the nameless servant as did Rebekah (Genesis 24:1-9). David cried out, "*God please, cleanse me with Hyssop. Return unto me the joy of my salvation. Take not thy Holy Spirit from me.*" (Psalm 51:7-12). That's how we have to be, because the only one who knows the way back home is the Holy Ghost.

I am conscious of what the Holy Spirit likes because I don't want to offend a dove that can and *will* fly away. The Lamb-like nature is being cultivated in me so that I can walk in the Spirit and not fulfill the lusts of the flesh. We don't follow the dictates of the flesh. If you live after the flesh you shall die, but if you through the spirit do mortify or deaden the deeds of the body you shall live (Romans 8:13). Through the Holy Spirit and the power given to us we are actually deadening the Adamic nature, the deeds of the flesh. Sin won't have dominion over me because I'm not under the law. All the flesh understands is rules and regulations.

The spiritual man is seeking transformation as it is renewed day by day. One person is trying to work his way in while another is dying and resurrecting their way in. Do you see how the two things are diametrically opposed one to the other? You have a Jehovah's Witness walking around door-to-door trying to earn his way into Heaven. While they are knocking at my door, I am sitting here sipping a glass of lemonade and reading the Bible as a child of God. I don't have to earn anything as I have received salvation as a gift of God.

The world won't like you because you came out of Egypt, but do not worry for you are not privy or subject to them any longer. You won't even have the desire for the things of the world like you used to. Not because you are forcing yourself not to, but because you no longer have the nature which desires those things. If there are others who are still bound by the world, challenge them to move up in Christ, but don't you take that old man down from the cross to be where they are. Remember these three things:

1. God gave His only begotten Son so that whosoever believes on Him should not perish, but have everlasting life. God did this for us while we were yet sinners. Through your own free will, you can repent and receive the sacrifice of Jesus Christ. This opens the door to salvation for you.

2. Through a process of sanctification, God enters into you and begins to make you as He is. He sanctifies and cleanses you; washes and regenerates you. He transforms you to make

you new by regenerating you through the Holy Ghost. He is producing in you a temple in which He can live.

3. Once He has a renovated temple, out of your belly will flow rivers of living water in order to generate life in others.

God does something **for** you, in order to do something **in** you, so that He can then flow **through** you. When He flows through you, you will know that you have arrived in the Promised Land; a land flowing with milk and honey. Living water flows through me and as a result, others are being saved, delivered, healed and restored. Demon-possessed people are having unclean spirits cast out so that they may be restored to their right minds. Blind eyes are being opened. The sick are being healed.

Take heed. On an Exodus, anyone can stop along the journey. However, you want to keep moving until you reach the Promised Land. According to the word of God, perilous times have come; these dangerous times are upon us now. The very culture of the world testifies to the fact that we are in the end times because those who are demon-possessed have a love affair with death. The expressions of this culture reflect a glorification of that which is dead: from the depiction of skulls and bones as a fashion trend, to shows which focus on zombies, vampires, werewolves, serial killers, murders, etc.

Why is this happening? The Devil is preparing people for the mass extermination of Christians (Revelation 11:7, 13:7). Before this can happen, he has to desensitize the world to death and create a thirst for bloodletting so that there will be no uproar or shock in response to these actions.

How do you think you could have 20,000 people sitting in a Roman Coliseum cheering while Christians were eaten alive by lions? Don't be deceived into thinking that a human being could not be reduced to that. They gnashed upon Stephen with their teeth as they tore at his flesh, and these were those who claimed to believe in God (Acts 7:54-57)! You had better know that the human heart is held back by the power of God from being as debased and vicious as it could be without Him (2 Thessalonians 2:6-7). God is restraining the realities of the fallen nature and what man can really become apart from Him because He is giving man time to repent. When He removes His hand you're going to see how far man can go into the depths of Satan. We have never seen this, but can get glimpses of it from history. One example is Adolf Hitler, who not even a century ago raised up a nation of people who watched him butcher 6 million people. He killed with impunity and virtually the entire nation helped him, either directly or through their silence.

In the days to come, most professing Christians will fall away and return

120

to Egypt because of what is about to happen in the earth. They will willingly choose to submit to the Devil instead of the authority of God as a means to escape the pressures and persecution coming our way. The Bible speaks of an economic crisis where you will not be able to buy or sell without the mark of the beast (Revelation 13:17). It speaks of children turning against parents, and brothers against sisters, as people offer you up to death in order to save their own lives (Matthew 10:17-36; Luke 12:51-53). This is why the devil has been preaching a watered-down Gospel message; so that you will not be prepared to stand.

Look for WWIII to break out and catastrophic natural disasters to increase. Expect to see the culmination of this religious ecumenical movement that is joining together the world's religions. Can't you see how the tide is turning? Now, it is widely believed that religion is the cause of all world problems, causing hatred, disparity, and intolerance. Religion is the obstacle preventing world peace and must be eliminated. We are living in the days where simply standing for the truths of God's word will have you labeled as a hater. Remember, there are 7 years of tribulation before the coming of Christ, but the first 3½ are not volatile. Those are the set-up years where the Devil is securing his plan and establishing what is needed for the ride of the Anti-Christ, who is not revealed until the mid-point of the tribulation.

We had better get ready by going on an Exodus. If you knew that destruction was coming to Sodom and Gomorrah, don't you think it would have made sense to leave? Think about it. If fire from Heaven is expected in the next 1½ hours, we could be at least 60 miles from here if we get in the car and push the pedal to the metal. This is the type of urgency we need to have because time is winding down.

Buddy, I am moving on. It is time for an exodus of my inner man. I need to disconnect from the world, seal my soul with the Holy Ghost, and lock into Christ, who is alone our source of power. I need to be so deep into Christ that all people see is Him and not me. Then, whatever He tells me to do, I will do. I am not just verbally confessing that I love the Lord, but I can walk in obedience, the evidence or fruit of that love. All God wants from man is obedience to His Spirit. The Holy Ghost is the angel leading God's people into the Promised Land. Obey what He tells you to do and you will not only be safe, but you will prosper.

Prosperity is not what most people say it is. Prosperity is being in the will of God and knowing that all He has for you will be accomplished as you walk in obedience to Him. Stephen was prosperous in the Lord, but it is not a prosperity that many will want to acknowledge. If we want to see where we are headed, we just need to look at Stephen.

Remember where we started in the beginning of the book. There are two seeds planted in this earth: the seed of the woman (who is Christ) and the seed of the serpent. One produces a martyr and the other produces a murderer. Those who are truly born again by incorruptible seed and manifested as a son of God will be martyrs. Those who are of the serpent's seed - including false religion - will be murderers. This is what we see as the religious leaders confront Stephen in the book of Acts.

Stephen is preaching about Jesus Christ and the Scripture says, "*And Stephen, full of faith and power, did great wonders and miracles among the people.*" (Acts 6:8). This is where we need to be; full of faith and power because we have been recreated in the image of Jesus Christ. Stephen was a manifested son of God. As evidence of the new life within him, God confirmed his words with miracles and signs following.

Various religious leaders disputed Stephen's testimony about Christ and had him called up before the synagogue's council to give an account of himself. Acts Chapter 7 relays to us Stephen's response. Notice that what Stephen says reinforces what has been outlined in this book. It is all about an exodus into the Promised Land.

Acts 7:1-60
*Then said the high priest, Are these things so? And he [Stephen] said, Men, brethren, and fathers, hearken; The God of glory appeared unto our father Abraham, when he was in Mesopotamia, before he dwelt in Charran, And said unto him, **Get thee out of thy country**, and from thy kindred, and **come into the land which I shall shew thee**. Then came he out of the land of the Chaldaeans, and dwelt in Charran: and from thence, when his father was dead, he removed him into this land, wherein ye now dwell. And he gave him none inheritance in it, no, not so much as to set his foot on: yet he promised that he would give it to him for a possession, and to his seed after him, when as yet he had no child.*

*And God spake on this wise, That his seed should sojourn in a strange land; and that they should bring them into bondage, and entreat them evil four hundred years. And the nation to whom they shall be in bondage will I judge, said God: and after that **shall they come forth, and serve me in this place. And he gave him the covenant of circumcision:** and so Abraham begat Isaac, and circumcised him the* *eighth day; and Isaac begat Jacob; and Jacob begat the twelve patriarchs.*

And the patriarchs, moved with envy, sold Joseph into Egypt: but God was with him, And delivered him out of all his afflictions, and gave him favour and wisdom in the sight of Pharaoh king of Egypt; and he made him governor over Egypt and all his house. Now there came a dearth over all the land of Egypt and Chanaan, and great affliction: and our fathers found no sustenance. But when Jacob heard that there was corn in Egypt, he sent out our fathers first. And at the second time Joseph was made known to his brethren; and Joseph's kindred was made known unto Pharaoh. Then sent Joseph, and called his father Jacob to him, and all his kindred, threescore and fifteen souls. So Jacob went down into Egypt, and died, he, and our fathers, And were carried over into Sychem, and laid in the sepulchre that Abraham bought for a sum of money of the sons of Emmor the father of Sychem.

But when the time of the promise drew nigh, which God had sworn to Abraham, the people grew and multiplied in Egypt, Till another king arose, which knew not Joseph. The same dealt subtilly with our kindred, and evil entreated our fathers, so that they cast out their young children, to the end they might not live. In which time Moses was born, and was exceeding fair, and nourished up in his father's house three months: And when he was cast out, Pharaoh's daughter took him up, and nourished him for her own son. And Moses was learned in all the wisdom of the Egyptians, and was mighty in words and in deeds. And when he was full forty years old, it came into his heart to visit his brethren the children of Israel. And seeing one of them suffer wrong, he defended him, and avenged him that was oppressed, and smote the Egyptian: For he supposed his brethren would have understood how that God by his hand would deliver them: but they understood not. And the next day he shewed himself unto them as they strove, and would have set them at one again, saying, Sirs, ye are brethren; why do ye wrong one to another? But he that did his neighbour wrong thrust him away, saying, Who made thee a ruler and a judge over us? Wilt thou kill me, as thou diddest the Egyptian yesterday? Then fled Moses at this saying, and was a stranger in the land of Madian, where he begat two sons.

*And when forty years were expired, there appeared to him in the wilderness of mount Sina an angel of the Lord in a flame of fire in a bush. When Moses saw it, he wondered at the sight: and as he drew near to behold it, the voice of the Lord came unto him, Saying, I am the God of thy fathers, the God of Abraham, and the God of Isaac, and the God of Jacob. Then Moses trembled, and durst not behold. Then said the Lord to him, Put off thy shoes from thy feet: for the place where thou standest is holy ground. I have seen, I have seen the affliction of my people which is in Egypt, and I have heard their groaning, and am come down to deliver them. And now come, I will send thee into Egypt. This Moses whom they refused, saying, Who made thee a ruler and a judge? The same did God send to be a ruler and a deliverer by the hand of the angel which appeared to him in the bush. **He brought them out, after that he had shewed wonders and signs in the land of Egypt,** and in the Red sea, and in the wilderness forty years.*

*This is that Moses, which said unto the children of Israel, A prophet shall the Lord your God raise up unto you of your brethren, like unto me; him shall ye hear. This is he, that was in **the church in the wilderness** with the angel which spake to him in the mount Sina, and with our fathers: who received the lively oracles to give unto us: To whom our fathers would not obey, but thrust him from them, and in their hearts turned back again into Egypt, Saying unto Aaron, Make us gods to go before us: for as for this Moses, which brought us out of the land of Egypt, we wot not what is become of him. And **they made a calf in those days, and offered sacrifice unto the idol, and rejoiced in the works of their own hands.** Then God turned, and gave them up to worship the host of heaven; as it is written in the book of the prophets, O ye house of Israel, have ye offered to me slain beasts and sacrifices by the space of forty years in the wilderness? Yea, ye took up the tabernacle of Moloch, and* *the star of your god Remphan, figures which ye made to worship them: and I will carry you away beyond Babylon.*

*Our fathers had the tabernacle of witness in the wilderness, as he had appointed, speaking unto Moses, that he should make it according to the fashion that he had seen. Which also our fathers that came after brought in with Jesus into the possession of the Gentiles, whom God drave out before the face of our fathers, unto the days of David; Who found favour before God, and desired to find a tabernacle for the God of Jacob. But Solomon built him an house. **Howbeit the most High dwelleth not in temples made with hands;** as saith the prophet, Heaven is my throne, and earth is my footstool: what house will ye build me? Saith the Lord: or what is the place of my rest? Hath not my hand made all these things?*

*Ye stiffnecked and uncircumcised in heart and ears, **ye do always resist the Holy Ghost**: as your fathers did, so do ye. Which of the prophets have not your fathers persecuted? And they have slain them which shewed before of the coming of the Just One; of whom ye have been now the betrayers and murderers: Who have received the law by the disposition of angels, and have not kept it. When they heard these things, they were cut to the heart, and **they gnashed on him with their teeth.** But he, **being full of the Holy Ghost, looked up stedfastly into heaven, and saw the glory of God, and Jesus standing on the right hand of God,** And said, Behold, I see the heavens opened, and the Son of man standing on the right hand of God. Then they cried out with a loud voice, and stopped their ears, and ran upon him with one accord, And cast him out of the city, and stoned him: and the witnesses laid down their clothes at a young man's feet, whose name was Saul. And they stoned Stephen, calling upon God, and saying, **Lord Jesus, receive my spirit**. And he kneeled down, and cried with a loud voice, Lord, lay not this sin to their charge. And when he had said this, he fell asleep.*

Being in communion with God required an exodus into the Promised Land, both from Abraham as well as his seed. Both Abraham and his seed had to be circumcised whereby they would be made separate and distinct from the demonic tribes around them, enabling them to bring forth uncontaminated life. Yet the church in the wilderness became overcome with idolatry because their hearts still longed for Egypt. As a result, many did not make it into the Promised Land. God brought them into this land with the goal of establishing a temple not made by human hands.

We are that temple. God desires for us to go on an exodus out from the world, through the Wilderness of Sin where we can be proven before inheriting His promises. What is that promise? That the Father and the Son will make their home in us - and us in them - because we have been organically grown to be a temple of God.

John 14:21-23
*He that hath my commandments, and keepeth them, he it is that loveth me: and he that loveth me shall be loved of my Father, and **I will love him, and will manifest myself to him**. Judas saith unto him, not Iscariot, Lord, how is it that thou wilt manifest thyself unto us, and not unto the world? Jesus answered and said unto him, If a man love me, he will keep my words: and my Father will love him, and **we will come unto him, and make our abode with him**.*

Stephen relays to us the pattern of manifestation. We must become an organically grown son of God by the Holy Spirit, manifesting the life of Jesus Christ to a dying world. Doing so requires us to go on an exodus away from time and space into the Spirit. In doing so, we leave behind the crucified old man and all of his ways. We proceed with circumcised hearts unto sanctification so that we can submit to God's will and not be pulled by the lusts of the flesh. We enter the Promised Land in the power of God, rending souls from Satan's kingdom.

What was the difference between Stephen and the religious leaders? They do always resist the Holy Ghost! They **resisted** the Holy Ghost while Stephen **submitted** to the Holy Ghost. The Holy Ghost was not living in them, but Stephen was full of the Holy Ghost. They walked about in their own authority and power while Stephen walked in the authority and power of God. This is why they hated Stephen; he was accepted and approved by God and they were not. This is what we are coming down to; the contrast between those who are truly sons of God and those who are merely bastards (Hebrews 12:8).

What can we expect at that point? Just look at Stephen. The response to his statements were vicious as they gnashed at his flesh with their teeth before stoning him to death. Yet even then he was not moved. He remained full of the Holy Ghost and His eyes singularly focused on Christ even in his hour of death. He died as a martyr for Christ; that is the definition of a witness, a "martyr". Do you want to be a witness for Christ? Then you too need to go on an exodus. You need to seek and submit to the organic life that God is creating in you by the Holy Spirit as He molds you into the image of His Son.

There is no argument to be had with what I'm saying; no need to go back and forth debating doctrine. People know instinctively that this is true. We must invoke the power of God in our lives in order to be representatives of Christ on this planet until we leave here.

What is God after all along the trail? He is after Jesus Christ formed in us; a people in whom the organic Gospel has produced resurrection life within, reconciling us to the Father and manifesting us to the world as sons so that we may bear fruit for His Kingdom.

Prayer

Father we thank you for the word of God, which is able to save our souls. We commit the time taken to read this book to you, asking that you bless our minds to understand your word and walk therein. God, change us into the image of your Son Jesus Christ. Take us on this Exodus. Move us from the outer court through the inner court into the Holy of Holies. Take us from the flesh, through the soul, and into the spirit. Create in us a clean heart and renew a right spirit within all of us.

Lord, I am praying for my mind. I am praying not to go insane and fall prey to the Devil's delusions. Don't let me give up in the midst of all this or be distracted away from my own salvation. People can say all of the religious jargon that they like about how God will keep you apart from your own will, but you said we must press in. We must strive to enter in through the strait gate because many will seek to enter in and will not be able to. There is a narrow way to life which few find, but a broad way to eternal damnation which many will choose. You instruct us to make our calling and election sure, because tomorrow is not promised to us. We must be ready to leave here every day, for no man knows the day or hour when his time has come.

God, this is a desperate thing, and we desperately need help to make it. I'm not taking anything for granted. Pride will take things for granted, but we need you God to keep us, to console us, to direct us and to convict us of sin that we might turn away from every evil way in Jesus' name. Amen.